Demonic County Durham:
Axe Murder in Ferry-Hill near Durham, 1682

Darrell S. Nixon

The Author would like to express his gracious thanks to everyone involved in providing
information and pictures to this book.

You can check out my other works:

www.DarrellSNixon.com

***

To K. D.
Thank you for listening.

Contents

Acknowledgements
The Devil you know

Many, Many Thanks...

In the writing of this book, there are a great number of people whom I need to give my utmost appreciation for their kindness and support, and the use of their material. This book would not be written without you.

- My family and friends;
- Mr Geoff Wall, Historian and Treasurer of the Ferryhill History Society;
- John Malkin, Ferryhill Facts newspaper;
- Maz Fentiman, @ Blackstar2302.deviantart.com;
- Nathan Cox, @ The-Screaming-Cat.Deviantart.com;
- Josh Fritz, model in "Zombie Apocalypse: Woodcutter" by Nathan Cox (as above);
- Graeme Pattison @newcastlemale.deviantart.com;
- Scott Robinson, Librarian, Member's Support at County Hall, Durham;
- Alison Brook of Clayport Library, Durham City;
- Durham University Archives and Special Collections;
- Liz Bragazzi, County Archivist of Durham County Record Office and the Incumbent Parish of Merrington;
- Jackie Brown, permissions manager of the British Library;
- Amy Gregor, Content Development Manager, Findmypast Newspaper Archive Limited;
- Ian Arkle, Communities Content Editor, Johnston Press North East;
- Maureen Anderson, author of many ghastly tales of County Durham,
- Ben Race of Capture Films, Newton Aycliffe;
- Chris Lloyd, Chief Editor of the Northern Echo;
- And lastly to my readers whoever you may be. Thank you for purchasing this book, I hope you enjoy it.

Introduction
Talk of the Devil

Ferryhill Facts, April/May 1989 — Page 2

Ferryhill Legends - THE MILLS MURDERS

I have long been aware that a legend exists in Ferryhill of a Spectre which haunts certain areas around new year, yet until recently the details had eluded me. Now, thanks to Geoff Wall (see page 14). I can tell the story of Andrew Mills to those who, like me, were curious but uninformed!

Andrew Mills, infact, was a young farm labourer on the farm of Tom and Mary Brass on the ridge to the west of the village near Kirk Merrington. Although normally a quiet youth, Mills gamed his notoriety in an act of violence which he was later to attribute to evil visions which guided his actions. Actions which were to have a dramatic effect on the village and the inhabitants for many years to come.

The story is centred on the 2nd January 1683, when Tom and Mary Brass went off to visit friends in the village, leaving their three children John aged 17, Jane aged 13, and Elizabeth aged 10, at home in bed. Not long after they had left, Andrew Mills burst into the house carrying a large carving knife and looking in a frenzied and posessed state. Disturbed by the noise, John, followed by Elizabeth, went to investigate, and ordered Mills to leave the house immediately. Mills, however leapt forward and killed John, causing Elizabeth to turn and flee back to her bedroom. Mills followed, and attacked her, trapping her arm in the door and breaking it. He then stabbed her to death, and cut her throat. Turning his attention to Jane, who lay terrified on her bed, Mills explained later that though he had always been fond of the child, he was forced to ignore her pleadings for mercy when a vision of a wolf with "fiery eyes and Eagle's wings" came to him as he began to back out of the room.

According to Mills testimony, the beast urged him "GO BACK THOU HATEFUL WRETCH, RESUME THY CURSED KNIFE - I LONG TO VIEW MORE BLOOD. SPARE NOT THE YOUNG ONE'S LIFE". With that, he rushed forward and killed the little girl. In a newspaper report of the time (Palatine. Durham. January 25th 1682) it was announced that "the children had been barbarously and inhumanly murdered; their throats being cut and their bodies mangled especially about the heads and the necks. Two axes were found, all bloody both the heads and the handles".

It was an hour later that Mr and Mrs Brass, on returning home, were alarmed when their horse stopped as if frightened, and refused to move further. From a nearby thicket, Mills, in a demented state, shouted out the dreadful details of what he had done, and then fled. He was persued by a company of troops, ultimately caught, and despite his obvioues insanity, condemned to death. His death was slow and agonising, with Mills being hung up in an iron cage at a sport near the farm. Legend has it that his cries - and that of the dogs howling - could be hear for miles, causing many to leave the area until it was all over. It is also said that a young servant girl from a nearby farm stayed with thim, feeding him milk through the bars until he finally died with a shriek which was as horrifying as it was loud. His body was hung on a gibbet for public exhibition, and that gibbet remained for years until it was ultimately cut up and sold for souveneirs and charms. Since then, it is said that his wild cries can still be heard in the are around the farmhouse at new year.

FERRYHILL FACTS COMMUNITY NEWSPAPER (ISSUE No 3), 1989,
(COURTESY OF JOHN MALKIN)

So you have decided to buy a book called '*Demonic* County Durham'. You are either wanting to find out about the darker side of County Durham's history, a keen reader of the supernatural, a friend of the author and you want to find out what I have written, or you just want a good read. At any rate, you are in good hands.

I will say however I am no storyteller when it comes to national or local history, or the paranormal. I deal with cold hard facts and logic. If you want a story, I suggest you end this now and read one of your favourite novels, but if you are like me, please read on as it may provide you with the same interest that has consumed my research for over 20 years, and hopefully give you some wisdom on how to deal with man's worst enemies - the Devil and himself.

In the 17th century, Europe, particularly those areas controlled by the English crown, was full of dealings with Satan and his demons. At every turn there was trials of witches and werewolves. There were masses of reported haunted places and buildings. There were people believing that they were bewitched, cursed, oppressed, or worse, possessed by forces of evil. Were these purely a mass state of mind within the environment, or possibly worse? People back then really believed that these forces were real, that the legions of hell and its supporters really walked upon the earth, and it was in man's best interest to be aware and prepare for any onslaught that was to come. These feelings were further overshadowed by premonitions, ill omens, and an end of the world, their world.

Being from Ferryhill, County Durham, I have always been fascinated by the town's local history, particularly certain events that are a mystery. The Ferryhill farmhouse murders in 1683 are one of them. My research into the local history came about when I came across a community newspaper written in 1989, called '*Ferryhill Facts*', and within one of the issues there was mentioned the murder. Since then I have always wanted to investigate the murders myself. Not content with one sample of the story, I wanted to find out what was truth and what was legend, and I gathered a great deal of information from libraries, book stores, and archives, trying ever hard to get at the bottom of why the murder took place.

This murder took place in a quiet neighbourhood and the servant Andrew Mills showed no provocation prior to the event. It was said that some terrible and diabolical force drove the young man to kill his employer's three children in the twilight hours of January 25th, 1683. If you have been or are a resident in Ferryhill or County Durham, you may be already aware of some of this information contained within, but even though you not local to this story, I welcome you to read my first book, this book.

In it, you will find all of the facts and legends placed in relevant order, and discover some new information that has never been known to the public before. Much of this would not be possible without the kind consents as mentioned in my acknowledgements. So prepare a warm drink (or a cold drink if you like), dim the lights, take a comfortable seat, get cosy, and prepare to read one of the most horrid and perplexing murders in this county's history, and why in 2016, 333 years since the event, it still has the same level of intense horror and intrigue as if it happened recently, and is still an area for discussion, even if it's a hushed one. Did the Devil really come to Ferryhill? Was it the cause for such a catastrophe?

I leave you with this introductory poem that I have made for such an occasion, and please enjoy the rest of the book.

Get you out from the bitter cold,
And listen at this tale from days of old.
When people were afraid of the darkest powers
Of the Devil and demons and whom they may devour.

"Once upon a time", as the old books say,
There once lived a family, small, but gay,
A mother and a father, and their three little lambs
In a farm on a hill, surrounded by lands.

Their happy lives would seem to last forever,
With the equal love they shared for each other.
Until one day, the father said,
"We need extra help to bring in our bread."

So the father went afar, so cheery and planned,
Into the city, to choose the right man,
And bring them back to all that would see
Who the new member of the house it would be.

And so begins this lamentable woe,
Of death, grief and despair also.
On stilly nights the warm heart stills,
When you hear this tale of Andrew Mills...

Part One

'A moth it is to trouble the mind's eye'

Prologue

The 'Hamlet' Prophecy

During the departing years of Queen Elizabeth I, a great poet by the name of William Shakespeare set to work in writing one of his most darkness plays – 'The Tragedy of Hamlet'. It is a tragic tale of plot, revenge, madness and murder. It was written sometime between 1599 and 1602, and was first performed to the public in 1603. Within the story, Heratio, the friend of the prince, informs us of the events leading to the assassination of Julius Caesar, and compares the event to the murder of his late King.

Neither did the character nor the playwright know that in a few years, the Stuart dynasty would begin and those same words seem to predict the forthcoming horrid "century of troubles" ....

'In the most high and palmy state of Rome'

- England was built upon the foundations of Roman invasion and occupation. In 55 B.C. and 54 B.C. Romans under the rule of Julius Caesar invaded Britain, but was unsuccessful and his army returned to Rome.
- In 45 B.C. Caesar becomes 'virtual dictator' of Rome and introduces the Julian calendar.
- Julius Caesar was assassinated in 44 B.C.
- England was left alone for almost a century, until the Romans invaded once again in 43 A.D, led by Claudius, and the Romans finally settled in England until 426 A.D. when Valentinian III withdraws all his troops.
- It was during the Roman occupation that London was formed in 49 A.D.

'A little ere the mightiest Julius fell'

- 1649 saw the collapse of the mighty crown of England, by the execution of Charles I.
- Between 1649 and 1660 saw the Commonwealth of England.

'The graves stood tenantless and the sheeted dead did squeak and gibber in the Roman streets'

- Between 1348 and 1349 the Black Death first swept across England. The population was close to 4 million and it swept away half.
- The Black Death revisited England in 1361, 1369, and 1407, but plagues continued right until the 18th century.
- In 1599 the Black Death reached County Durham. In Ferryhill, between August and September of that year, twenty-six people died.
- Between 1664 and 1665, London was hit, and it swept away 40% of the city's population.

'As stars with trains of fire....'

- In October 1607, Halley's comet, named after Edmond Halley (1656 – 1742) was seen across the sky. The comet was next seen again in September 1682.
- In 1618, the Great Comet was visible to the naked eye.
- In 1661, a comet was observed by Johannes Hevelius (1611 – 1687)
- Between 1665 and 1666, two comets were seen, and there was also an eclipse of the moon.

'...and dews of blood'

- Between 1642 and 1651, there was bloody civil war in England between royalists and parliamentarians. An estimate of 100,000 people died due to war-induced disease and over 84,500 people died of the war itself. The estimate total dead gives a staggering 190,000 people out of five million English people (3.8%).
- In 1658 saw the "Battle of the Dunes", in Dunkirk, which was part of the Spanish Netherlands, now France. It was an alliance between Parliamentarian England (Oliver Cromwell) and France (Cardinal Richelieu) against the Spanish army and the English Royalists and French Fronde rebels.

'Disasters in the sun and the moist star'

- In 1607, Bristol suffered a massive flood, which resulted in the drowning of approximately 2000 people, and it swept away houses and villages over an area of 200 square miles. Livestock and farmland was saturated, destroying the local economy.
- Between 1608 and 1692, there were approximately 8 earthquakes recorded in the British Isles. The Richter scales of each earthquake were recorded from 4.7 and 5.8
- The drought between 1665 and 1665, increased the death count of the Great Plague of London, and allowed the fire of the Great Fire of London to spread more rapidly and easily.

'Upon whose influence Neptune's empire stands'

- Neptune was the Roman God of the sea, and in art and sculpture, he is often seen as an old man with a trident in his hand. Neptune is symbolic of England.

'Was sick almost to doomsday with eclipse'

- The eclipses of the sun or moon were seen as terrifying omens, as they were often believed to mark the beginning of disasters.

Chapter 1
The Key Events of the Devil in the Early Stuarts

King James the Sixth of Scotland and First of England

- Born on 19 June 1566, the son of Henry Stuart of Lennox and Mary Queen of Scots
- Crowned King of Scotland on 24 July 1567, aged 13 months old, following the execution of his mother Mary Queen of Scots.
- Crowned King of England and Ireland (and union of Scotland and France) on 25 July 1603, aged 36 years old, following the death of Queen Elizabeth I.
- Died on 27 March 1625, aged 59 years old, succeeded by his second son, Charles I

James was already the Sixth of Scotland during the reign of Queen Elizabeth I, but following her death in 1603, there was no heir or sibling that could take the crown. It is understood Elizabeth I had wrote numerously appraising her young cousin James, the son of her cousin-once-removed, Mary Queen of Scots. Mary was earlier executed in 1567 on the orders of Queen Elizabeth for conspiring against her, and James, at such a young age, became James the VI of Scotland.

James had no personal memories of his mother Mary due to his early age of her death but he knew that following the death of his cousin Elizabeth that he had the most chance of succeeding to the throne. In 1603, James the VI of Scotland was crowned James I of England, Ireland and France.

'Daemonologie', King James VI and I, 1599

Published in 1599, '*Daemonologie*' was the only book fully written and sanctioned by James, and was heavily influenced by his personal involvement in the North Berwick witch trials in 1590, where it was mentioned that some women had attempted by use sorcery to founder a ship carrying him and his new wife, Anne of Denmark, to Scotland. Witch trials had been mostly confined to Scotland, but when James took the throne of England, his book, seemingly sanctioning the approval of witch hunting, swept over England like a virus.

Many witch hunters were created because of this, the most notable was Matthew Hopkins, who flourished between 1644 and 1647 as the Witchfinder General during the English Civil War. He and his associates were responsible for the deaths of well over a hundred people in the southern parts of England.

The Divine Right of Kings

James believed in the absolute divine rule of his kingdoms, by will of God alone. This medieval belief of divine right meant that the monarchy was not subject to no earthly authority: the will of the people, the aristocracy, estate of the realm such as Parliament. This led him with indifference to many religious groups, and later to conspiracies of murder and usurp of the English throne.

Main Plot and Bye Plot of 1603

Even before James became the King of England, his succession to kingship was not safe. During the coronation preparation in July 1603, there was an alleged plot by English courtiers to remove him from the English throne and replace him with his cousin, Arabella Stuart, who was first thought initially to be the successor of her cousin Queen Elizabeth I. Arabella Stuart was believed to have sympathies with Spain, who had tried and failed to invade the English kingdom in August 1588, via the Spanish Armada. This was known as the Main Plot.

The Bye Plot was an alleged conspiracy by Roman Catholic priests and puritans to kidnap James (within the Main Plot) due to the religious constraints placed under them by the Acts of Parliament, which informed them that they had to worship by the rules of the Church of England and to use the Common Prayer Book.

In November and December of 1603, many of the Priest conspirators were tried and executed, and some of those involved in the Main Plot were placed in the tower of London, which included Arabella Stewart, and Sir Walter Raleigh.

The Witchcraft Act of 1604

Henry VIII first introduced the Witchcraft Act of England in 1542 and its supposed use was deemed a capital, punishable offence. The Act was further changed in 1563, and was less merciful that its predecessor, as any persons believed to involved in the use of magic or sorcery would only be tried by the Church and punished if it could be proved that witchcraft was used to harm or murder someone.

No sooner after becoming King of England and Ireland, James set to work in repealing and completely changing the existing Witchcraft Law of the late Queen, and how persons involved in sorcery would be punished. Between 1604 and 1735 the Common Court would try anyone who was accused of being in league with the Devil and was using witchcraft or sorcery. They were tortured, even to bring about a false confession, and executed.

This change in the law caused massive injustice to the lives of the people under his reign. It was the cause of many witch trials, the execution by hanging of innocent men and women, and the cause of fear and superstition against the practices of herbal medicine, and old practices of healing.

The Gunpowder Plot of 1605

Once again tensions were building up regarding the reign and religious views of the new king. In the Midlands, a small group of Jesuits planned the murder of James and the blowing up of the House of Lords during the State Opening of Parliament on the 5 November 1605.

A member of the group called Guy Fawkes was set the task of setting up and setting off the gunpowder explosion below the parliament's foundations. However, their plot was foiled, and Guy Fawkes and many of the Jesuit group was executed for treason against the crown. We still refer to this event as 'Bonfire Night' or 'Guy Fawkes Night'.

The *King James Bible* was commissioned by James VI and I in 1604, and was published in 1611. It was to reflect the climate of current Christian values and to be used by ordained clergy in the Church of England. It was also a showcase masterpiece to reflect on his great intellect on God upon his subjects, and it was used as a primary source when dealing with the demonic. The King James Version is most common bible used across the world today.

Seventeenth century belief held that the Devil was a powerful adversary to God and to mankind, for it is said that God made man in *'His own image'*. According to the scriptures of the Bible, there are many versions of how the Devil came into being. He is initially is found in the Book of Genesis, when Eve was tempted by the serpent to eat the forbidden fruit on the tree of knowledge against the advice of God. In turn Eve tempted Adam to also eat the fruit, they were then both cast out from the Garden, and to live in constant torment in the current world.

In other scriptures of the Bible the Devil was originally an archangel (a high deity below God and his Son), was called Lucifer, and it is told that he became envious of Jesus Christ. He rose up with his sympathizers to try to reform the Governance of God in a heavenly war, which ended in God winning, and Lucifer and his supporters being cast down from Heaven and onto the Earth. Lucifer became the Devil and his supporters became demons. After this, God informed man to be wary of the Devil and his supporters in our presence:

'Be sober, be vigilant; because your adversary the devil, as a roaring lion, walketh about, seeking whom he may devour.' (Peter 5:8)

'Here is wisdom. Let him that hath understanding count the number of the beast: for it is a man; and his number is six hundred threescore and six [666]' (Revelations 13:18)

The Bible also states quite clearly that the Devil and his minions are not to be trusted:

'...for even Satan disguises himself as an angel of light' (Corinthians 11:14)

'Beloved, do not believe every spirit, but test the spirits to see whether they are from God, for many false prophets are gone into the world' (John 4:1)

The Bible also informs us that even after exorcism the person previously inflicted may not be free of the demons that possessed him:

'When the unclean spirit is gone out of a man, he walketh through dry places, seeking rest, and findeth none. Then he saith, I will return into my house from when I came out; and when he come, he findeth it empty, swept and garnished. Then goeth he, and taketh with himself seven other spirits more wicked than himself, and they enter in and dwell there; and the last state of that man is worse than the first...' (Matthew 12:43-45)

Charles the First

- Born on 19 November 1600, son of James VI and I and Anne of Denmark
- Crowned King on 2 February 1626, aged 25 years old
- Executed in public on 30 January 1649, aged 48 years old.

King James I died in 1625 and his son Charles, Duke of Albany, became King Charles I. Much like his father before him, Charles also believed in the divine right of rule, and he strongly believed that he had absolute right to govern his country by his own conscience. This brought him into conflict with the Government of England who sought to curb his authority and rights above the common law. His religious views were seen as too catholic in the eyes of his opponents, and in 1642, the English Civil War broke out.

The Execution of a King

Charles fought the English and Parliamentarian Armies, led by Oliver Cromwell. In 1645, he was defeated and surrendered to a Scottish force that eventually handed him over to the English parliament. Charles refused adamantly to a constitutional monarchy, and temporarily escaped his captors in November 1647. Found and imprisoned in the Isle of Wright, Charles tried to forge an alliance of Scotland, but by December 1648, the 'New Model Army' of Oliver Cromwell dominated its control over England. Charles was tried and convicted of high treason in January 1649, and on the 30th day of that same month, at 2.00 pm, Charles was executed.

He is the only sovereign in English history to be executed in a public spectacle, without a battle, and although the monarchy was restored in 1660, the royal governing powers of England was banished forever.

The Commonwealth of England

- Led by Oliver Cromwell, dictator, and 1st Lord Protector from 16 December 1653, aged 54 years old.
- England became under military rule.
- Oliver Cromwell died on 3 September 1658, aged 59 years old.
- His son, Richard, became the 2nd Lord Protector on 3 September 1658, aged 31 years, but due to his incapacity of governance of both parliament and the army, he was forcibly resigned in 1649, only serving 8 months.

After the execution of Charles I, a military republic was declared known as the "Commonwealth of England." The head of the Commonwealth was politician and Leader of the Independent Party, Oliver Cromwell. Cromwell was aware of the three difficulties ahead of him. There was dissatisfaction in his own army, the Royalists in Ireland, and the Royalists in Scotland.

The Royalists in Ireland

The Royalist army of Ireland consisted of Roman Catholic, Episcopalian and Presbyterian, *'all ready to shed their blood'* for the son of the late King. In 1649, Cromwell and his select army of ten thousand men rode into Ireland, and within nine months Cromwell had *'utterly broken the power of the Royalist army'*. His method was simple: that every town, village or city surrender to him immediately or be faced by storm and *'death to every man carrying arms'*.

The Royalists in Scotland

In 1649, the son of the executed Charles I was invited to reside in Scotland, and soon after he arrived. It was here where the young prince unhappily agreed, as part of his bargain for support, to sign the National Covenant of Scotland, a legal document which affirmed Scotland's loyalty to the king, but asserted its independence from English influence in church matters.

When Cromwell came to Scotland in 1650, a garrison of the Scottish Army in Dunbar cut the English army short in its tracks. Unfortunately, on 3 September, Cromwell took out the entire Dunbar section. Meanwhile, the young prince Charles chanced for a fortune in war and on New Year's Day in 1651 set off with his supporters to England and went as far as Worcester where on 28th August, he was hopelessly defeated by Cromwell.

With nowhere to go, and fearing the same fate of his father, the young prince *'cut off his long hair and wearing peasant clothing'* fled to into the English countryside. A reward of ten thousand pounds was offered for his apprehension. Feeling no longer safe in his once beloved kingdom he moved from Shropshire to Sussex, where he chanced to get on a coal vessel and made his way to Normandy, in France.

England under military rule

On 16 December 1653, Cromwell became 'Lord Protector of the Commonwealth of England, Scotland and Ireland', and England became a nation ruled by a puritan government and the army. The Church of England became puritan, and Anglican priests were replaced with puritan ministers.

The worship of Holy Days

It was during the Commonwealth that Christian practices and recreation were plunged into darkness. The puritan government believed that such events led to misrule, and so abolished the celebration of holy events, such as Christmas, Easter and other Saints days.

In 1580, puritan author Phillip Stubbes wrote in his book *'The Anatomie of Abuses'*:

> 'That more mischief is that time committed than in all the year besides, what masking and mumming, whereby robbery, whoredom, murder and what not is committed? What dicing and carding, what eating and drinking, what banqueting and feasting is the used, more than in all the year besides, to the great dishonour of God and impoverishing of the realm.'

English customs such as public drunkenness, dice and card games, theatres, taverns, cockfighting, bear baiting, and the making of specially brewed ales were all abolished in law. Wreaths on doors, and mince pies (all representing the Christ child in the manger) were opposed. Stores selling goods were ordered to be open on Christmas Day and people attending non-puritan festivals were fined.

The Death of Cromwell and the Commonwealth

Oliver Cromwell died on 3 September 1658, and the role of Lord Protector was passed on to his son Richard on the same day, but he lacked the authority presence over parliament and the army, unlike his father before him. By 25 May 1659, he was forcibly resigned.

Chapter 2
King Charles II: The Prince of Retribution

- Born on 29 May 1630, son of Charles I and Henrietta Maria of France
- Proclaimed King by the Scottish Parliament on 5 February 1649
- Defeated by Oliver Cromwell in the Battle of Worcester on 28 August 1651, and Charles II fled to mainland Europe.
- Restored to the throne on 29 May 1660, aged 30 years old
- Charles II died on 6 February 1685, aged 54 years old, and was succeeded by his brother James II.

Our story really begins on the restoration of the English crown. Charles II returned to London with great admiration and on 30 January 1660, was restored to the throne. His coronation was seen by many to be of a new era of *'happiness, prosperity and peace'*.

The new King was described as 'a man of great natural talents, an easy going and unruffled temper, and the most charming and attractive manners; but he had no principles and very little heart'. Under the guise of 'an idle and careless manner', he was determined to bring back the absolute power of the English Crown, and his first order of power was to remind England what holy power made him King, and who murdered his late father.

'Revenge his foul and most unnatural murther'

The Act of Indemnity of 1660

The Act of Indemnity of 1660 brought about the amnesty, return of property and the return and practices of an Anglican Church of England, which was controlled or made unlawful by the Commonwealth puritan government. However, those responsible for his late father's death were except from the Act and held accountable for their actions. The judges at his late father's trial were executed at Charing Cross, *'in sight of the place where they put to death their late and natural prince'*.

This Act not only referred to persons living, but to the dead. In an unanimous vote in the House of Commons, the bodies of Cromwell and others involved in the persecution and execution of Charles I were dragged from their tombs in Westminster Abbey, hung in chains on the common gallows at Tyburn Gate where they remained for an entire day, afterward their heads were beheaded and placed on pikes and their bodies were buried at the foot of the gallows, amongst the common thieves and murderers of the age.

The New Parliament and new Acts, 1661 to 1665

Charles II created a new parliament of 1661, which consisted of chief royalist politicians and clergymen. They began to create and pass Acts to control and maintain allegiance to the Crown and control the movement and actions of certain religious groups:

The Cooperation Act (or act of obedience to the Crown) in 1661.

This Act ensured that all magistrates and officials in the towns and cities of England to swear by passive obedience to the Crown, to renounce the Covenant of England, and to receive sacrament of an Anglican priest within one year before their election. They also had to send the King their official address of residence.

The Act of Uniformity (or act of religious doctrine) in 1662

This Act made it clear that all clergymen, fellow of a college and every schoolmaster to give his *'unfeigned assent and consent'* to every statement in the Book of Common Prayer and to take an oath that any resistance to the Crown was both sinful and unlawful.

The Conventicle Act (Act against the Gathering of Religious Groups) in 1664

This Act forbade the gathering of more than five people (other than members of the Church of England) for religious purposes, and forbade private family worship, which was punishable by transportation.

The Five Mile Act (or Act against unregistered clergymen) in 1665

This Act forbade any clergymen who did not subscribe to the Act of Uniformity or did not sign an oath of non-resistance to the King, coming or settling within a five-mile radius of any corporate town or city, or teaching in schools. This was punishable by a fine of £40 and six months imprisonment.

These four Acts were known as the *'Clarendon Code'* and the purpose was to place the Church of England in its previous position, before the time of the Commonwealth.

Bad Omens

The Great Plague of London 1665

In June 1665, the weather was noted as extremely hot and the winter and spring had been the driest time ever known in England. London was a growing city where the streets were narrow with the houses over hung onto the public street. There was mass overcrowding, and there was no clean and suitable sanitation system to clear away the human and animal pollution from the paths, roads, and waters. People became seriously ill as bacteria spread, and eventually led to one of the most recorded death toll in the great city. Samuel Pepys, the noted diarist of the time wrote *'Lord have mercy upon us'* and men driving carts went round London were noted as shouting *'Bring out your dead!'* The estimate death toll of London was approximately 10,000 people, an estimated quarter of London's inhabitants.

The Great Fire of London, 1666

On Sunday the 2nd of September 1666, at 3 o'clock in the morning, a housemaid of diarist Samuel Pepys stated that she had seen a blaze in London. Mr Pepys awakes from his bed, goes to her room, and upon looking out her window, sees the east end of London alight with flames.

However, Pepys thought the fire was too far off to care further, and went back to bed; only to be woken up a few hours later as the flames drew near.

The fire started in Pudding Lane in a baker's shop and ended four days later in the centre of London, taking with it 13,200 houses, 87 parish churches, St Paul's Cathedral and most of the buildings of the cities authorities. The new King was noted of attempting to put an end to the blaze by informing his ministers to gunpowder empty homes to prevent the spread of the fire. In the end when the fires ceased, amazingly there were only six deaths recorded, as many people had managed to escape by road or flee by boat in the Thames.

Political Works against the Crown

'Paradise Lost', 1667

John Milton, the noted poet and novelist, was a civil servant under the Commonwealth of England. Milton believed that the death of Charles I was right, due to he believing that the King had brought about the Civil War. He also believed in free speech. These matters did not bide well with the new king, and now upon the restoration, Milton went into hiding for his life after a warrant was made out for his arrest, and some of his writings were burnt. He re-emerged when he was later pardoned, but Milton and the King did not see 'eye to eye' and was arrested and imprisoned before one of his powerful friends, now a Member of Parliament, intervened.

In 1667, Milton, now blind, published his famous work, *'Paradise Lost'*, in which Satan decides to revolt against the reign of God in a heavenly civil war, and in the aftermath is thrown down to the Earth. Milton believed even though England needed a lawful King, no man, let alone a monarch, stands alone by the will of God, and should be instead ruled over by a group of men, where decisions are made unanimously for the good of the people, not by the good of the throne. It is a powerful story of the battle between good and evil, and 'Paradise Lost' stands today as an allegory for social justice.

Popish Plot, 1678

It would seem again that the throne of England was once again in danger. In September 1678, Charles II found out from a trial of a man called Titus Oates that there had been a conspiracy against his person. In a magistrate's court, Oates had alleged under oath that there existed an extensive catholic conspiracy to assassinate the King, and return England back to the time of puritan rule under the Commonwealth.

Although the supposed Popish Plot never went ahead, it did not prevent the King to protect himself. He used the confession of Oates and had twenty-two men executed who was said to be behind the plot.

Sibling War

Charles tried to bring about the Exclusion Act of 1681, which sought to exclude his brother James (later James II from 1685 to 1688) from the British crown because of his Roman Catholic religion. In 1681 the Act was defeated when it went into the House of Lords.

Chapter 3
'As harbingers preceding still the fates'

The County Palatine of Durham

Durham City under early Stuart reign

In the 17th century, Durham City was a small city nestled in the centre of a palatine county, within the North East of England.

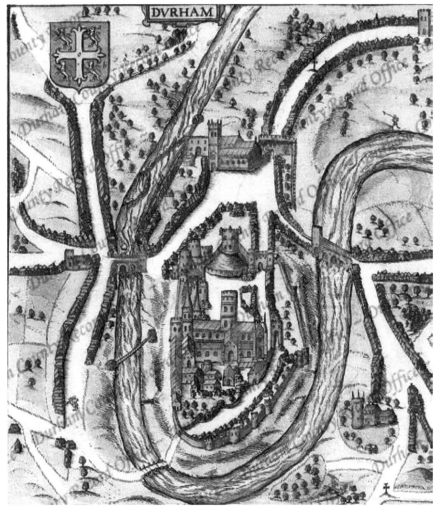

JOHN SPEED'S MAP OF DURHAM CITY, CIRCA 1611 (DRO D/XP 77)
(COURTESY OF DURHAM COUNTY RECORD OFFICE)

A map of Durham City dated 1611 by John Speed (DRO D/XP 77), shows in the centre of Durham the commanding building of the Cathedral and Castle, surrounded by the River Wear. Around the river was the old assize court on Palace Green, the North Gate prison which was once at the top of Saddler Street, the House of Correction at Elvet Street, and scattered around were trees and small churches, and on the old roads stood small and cramped houses. Durham was not only a place for residence, it was a place of pilgrimage for men who wish to visit the sacred body of Saint Cuthbert, whose body was brought from Lindisfarne into 'Dunholm' in 995 AD. It was recorded that women were able to enter the Cathedral, but not to the site of where St Cuthbert lay, as it was a common belief that the Saint did not care for the female sex. Such was society back then.

DURHAM CATHEDRAL VIEWED FROM FRAMWELLGATE BRIDGE
(AUTHOR'S PHOTOGRAPH)

The Cathedral held the 'Dean and Chapter'. This was an ecclesiastical body of bishops, whose responsibilities were to instruct holy prayer, but also to ensure that revenue were paid in from tenants of their lands. The Dean and Chapter was the body to which countrymen had to apply to excavate for coal and or any sort of use with their property.

Durham Castle was built in 1072 after the Norman Conquest, and it was here that on the 13th April 1603, King James the Sixth, whilst he was on his way to London to receive his British crown, stayed and was entertained by the Bishop and a hundred noblemen. Durham also played host to James on his way to Scotland in 1617, and once more, the castle again played host to James I's son, Charles I in 1633 upon his coronation, and in 1639 when the King marched against the Scottish Covenanters, during the English Civil War

DURHAM CASTLE VIEWED FROM FRAMWELLGATE BRIDGE
(AUTHOR'S PHOTOGRAPH)

After the execution of Charles I in 1649, Oliver Cromwell became the leader of the new Commonwealth, and it is in a letter dated 1650 that he favoured Durham as a place of learning for the poor and ignorant Northerners:

> 'A matter of great concernment and importance as that which (by the blessing of God) may much conduce to the promoting and learning and piety in these poore rude and ignorant partes, there being also many concurring advantages to this place, as pleasantness and aptness of scituation, healthful aire and plenty of provisions, which seems to favour and please for their desires therein.'

On 15 May 1657, Oliver Cromwell attempted to make a university in Durham, but Oxford and Cambridge Universities suppressed his actions on account of petitions. The castle at Durham only became part of Durham University in 1840.

Some curious facts of Durham are told in John Sykes *Local Records: Volume One*, in that in 1637, the steeple of the old church of St. Mary-le-Bow in Durham collapsed into the street two days after divine service was made, taking with it a great portion of the west side of the Church. The church lay in ruins until 1683 when sufficient funds were made to start restoration, which finished in 1685.

War was always on the political agenda in the 17th Century. In 1615, at Whitworth near Spennymoor, a muster of 8320 County Durham men between the ages of 16 and 60 were ordered to come together to bear arms. Durham City and its surrounding towns alone carried with it 560 men.

Durham City had already seen the great plague that had swept through England for most of the earlier centuries. In 1604, the plague was recorded in St Giles parish in Durham. It was the last of the plague within the city, which had occurred intermittently since 1589, and it took with it many of the county's inhabitants. In 1610, the plague was present again but in the town of Lumley, taking 78 people to the grave.

The Witchcraft Acts also had an impact on Durham. Between 1565 and 1668, eight women were tried as witches.

Durham City under Charles II

In the year 1682, a man called *Jacob Bee*, living in Durham City, is noted as marking some interesting entries within his diary. Although he may not have realised it, Jacob would be the backbone to chronicle the strange weather and events of that year. The first was to come in the form of floods:

> '1682 April. Two great floods of watter upon Wednesday and Thursday, being the 26th and 27th of April.'

The second would come in the form of thunder and lightning:

> '1682. 31 May. Betwixt 11 and 12 at night, was a very fearful thunder, with flashes of fire, very terrible'.

The third and final came in the form of Halley's comet.

'1682. 15 August. A blazing star appeared'

The Parish of Merrington

THE CHURCH AT KIRK MERRINGTON, WHICH WAS REMODELLED IN 1845
(AUTHOR'S PHOTOGRAPH)

Six miles south of Durham City on the old roman road, still stands the old parish church of Kirk Merrrington, Saint John the Evangelist.

The oldest record of the church was in 1143-4, when a Scottish intruder called William Cumyn tried to usurp of the Bishopric of Durham, by fortifying the church and manning the tower, but was driven out by three barons of the Bishopric. The fortification and his eventual surrender left the church roof destroyed but the rest of the building remained intact. He was apparently left mad after leaving the church.

The church tower features in the Battle of Neville's Cross in 1346 when it was used as an outlook post for the English army. The position of the church on the highest point of the hill meant that the soldiers could see literally for miles around, and could see the advance of the Scottish army.

The parish church of Kirk Merrington looked slightly different from how the church looks today. A beautiful illustration by Robert Billings in his book '*Architectural Antiquities of the County of Durham*' (1846) shows the tower of the church with its beautiful cornered points, and brickwork. The renovation of the church between 1850 and 1851 meant that the every stone of the church were almost removed, replaced, and enlarged to accommodate a flock of 300 persons. The renovation of the church also caused the majestic tower to be flattened, losing its incredible former beauty.

The parish of Merrington consisted of Hett, Ferryhill, Little Chilton and Great Chilton. The parish mostly consisted of agricultural workers, farmers, and innkeepers. The land was used for livestock such as sheep, cattle and oxen, and for harvesting hay, fruits and barley for drinking. Whilst private individuals owned some of the land, the Dean and Chapter of Durham owned most of the land and the properties therein.

Ferry-Hill, in the parish of Merrington

THE MANOR HOUSE AT FERRYHILL, NOW A HOTEL
(AUTHOR'S PHOTOGRAPH)

A mile and a half east of Kirk Merrington stands the small town of Ferry-Hill. Ferryhill, or 'Ferry-Hill' as it was called in the reign of Charles II, was a considerable smaller town than it is today. A map dated 1765, held in the archives of Durham University, shows the majority of the town houses were gathered up Durham Road, around Market Street, North Street and Main Street. Other houses were scattered along Merrington Road, Darlington Road, and Wood Lane. On this map, there appears to be a building where the Town Hall stands today, but the current town hall was built in 1886, meaning that a previous building stood on the same spot, and could have been the same type of focal point for the town.

The manor house at the back of North Road still exists in the town and is now a hotel. It was built in the latter part of the 16th century.

Ferryhill was mostly a quiet place, the only issues were petty crimes recorded in the Quarter Session books. It wasn't until the farmhouse murders in 1683 that Ferryhill was put firmly on the County Durham map and into the annals of history...

Part Two

'So shall you hear of carnal, bloody, and unnatural acts'

Illustrative map of Ferryhill, between 1600 and 1800

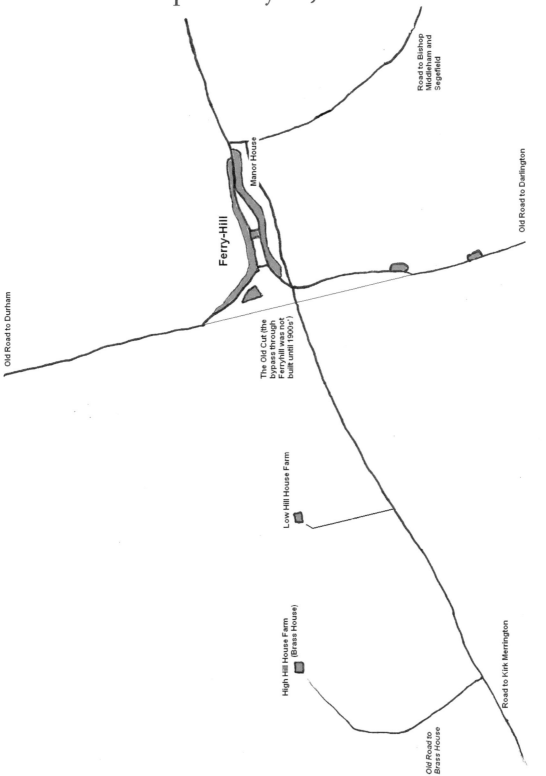

Road to Bishop Middleham and Segefield

Old Road to Darlington

Manor House

Ferry-Hill

Old Road to Durham

The Old Cut (the bypass through Ferryhill was not built until 1900s')

Low Hill House Farm

High Hill House Farm (Brass House)

Road to Kirk Merrington

Old Road to Brass House

Chapter 4
'Give order to these bodies high on a stage be placed to the view'

The Location

A farmhouse still stands high on the western ridge of Ferryhill called High Hill House Farm. In the late 17th century, the farmhouse was called Brass House and was tenanted from the Dean and Chapter of Durham by the respectable Brass family, who lived in their home since the baptism of their eldest child.

The Victims

The family consisted of husband and wife, John and Margaret Brass, with their three children, Jane, John and Elizabeth. Joined in the house was a young man, called Andrew Mills, who was servant to their father.

The Parents: John and Margaret Brass

- It is estimated that their marriage took place between 1650 and 1662. No official record of their marriage has yet been found.
- John and Margaret must have been in their fortieth or fiftieth years in 1683.
- Although not murdered, John and Margaret were also intended victims of the murderer four days before the actual event (21 January 1683).

The closest record I have come across for John and Margaret's wedding is recorded on the *FreeREG* website (which records parish records). A record exists that in 1656, in the place of Wymondham, parish of Reymerstone, Norfolk, within the Church of the Virgin Mary and St Thomas a Becket, a bachelor called "John Breese" and a spinster called "Margarett Hardy" was married in that year. Although we can never be sure that these are the same people, it is the closest to find in terms of names. If it is the same people, what made them decide to take up residence in the County of Durham?

Their first child: Jane Brass

- Baptised: Sunday, 22 February 1663, Kirk Merrington Church – 'Jane, daughter of John Brass of Ferryhill, baptised Feb 22, 1662' (DRO EP/Mer 1)
- Murdered: Thursday, 25 January 1683
- Age from baptism to death: 19 years, 11 months and 3 days (7,277 days from baptism) (www.Calculator.net)
- Date of Birth: Sunday, 25 January 1663 (Age from baptism add 28 days = 7,305 days) (www.timeanddate.com)
- Age from birth to death: 20 years exactly

In '*The Monthly Chronicle of North Country Lore and Legends: Volume One*' (1887), the author suggests that the eldest daughter Jane was:

> 'well fitted to play a woman's part in the peculiar work which then fell into a woman's share. While an adept in the duties of the kitchen, she would occasionally lend a hand to business, which more particularly pertained to the male portion of the household. There was, moreover, a dash of the heroic in her nature, combined, as it often is, with a full flow of animal spirits, rendered brighter by perfect health, and made temptingly beautiful by an archness of manners which tantalised the young farmers who spent evenings at the Hill House...Jane was not long to waste her young years in single wretchedness, looking after her mother's dairy and making the farm-house nice and clean – a beacon to all the young swains of the neighbourhood. She had already given her heart and hand to one who was worthy of both.'

Jane was due to be married on Candlemas, on the 2nd February 1683.

Their second child: John Brass (the younger)

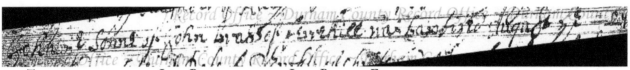

THE BAPTISM RECORD OF JOHN BRASS, THE SON OF JOHN BRASS OF FERRYHILL FROM THE PARISH REGISTER
OF KIRK MERRINGTON, (DRO EP/MER 1)
(COURTESY OF DURHAM RECORD OFFICE AND THE INCUMBENT PARISH OF MERRINGTON)

- Baptised: Tuesday, 29 August 1665, Kirk Merrington Church – 'John, ye sonne of John Brass of Ferryhill, baptised Aug 29, 1665' (DRO EP/Mer 1)
- Murdered: Thursday, 25 January 1683
- Age from baptism to death: 17 years, 4 months and 27 days (6,358 days from baptism) (www.Calculator.net)
- Date of Birth: Wednesday, 25 January 1665 (Age from baptism add 7 months and 3 days = 18 years) (www.timeanddate.com)
- Age from birth to death: 18 years exactly

In *'The Monthly Chronicle of North Country Lore and Legends: Volume One'* (1887), the author described the son John as lacking the will and determination of his eldest sister Jane, in that he:

> 'manifested a weak and easy character. He was valuable in carrying out orders in which he was able to perform, but he could neither devise nor execute on his own account. His father was blind to his faults – indeed, rather liked them – for few fathers in those days, any more than in the present, cared to see a spirit in their sons which too soon showed itself independent of parental control.'

Their third child: Elizabeth Brass

- Baptised: Tuesday, 13 February 1672, Kirk Merrington Church – 'Elizabeth, daughter of John Brass of Ferryhill, baptised Feb 13, 1671' (DRO EP/Mer 2)
- Murdered: Thursday, 25 January 1683
- Age from baptism to murdered: 10 years, 11 months and 12 days (3,999 days from baptism) (www.Calculator.net)
- Date of Birth: Thursday, 25 January 1672 (Age from baptism add 19 days= 4018 days) (www.timeanddate.com)
- Age from birth to death: 11 years exactly

In '*The Monthly Chronicle of North Country Lore and Legends: Volume One*' (1887), the author described the youngest daughter Elizabeth, the youngest child, as so full of character:

> '...Mrs Brass had another daughter, Elizabeth, aged eleven, gradually coming up to take the place of her who was soon to enter upon a new world of interests and responsibilities. Elizabeth was a lively, rural maiden, somewhat saucy, as maidens about her age generally are, but kind hearted and wise above her years.'

'Star crossed' birthdays

If the birth dates are indeed correct, it would reveal one the most interesting facts of the children that has never been previously known – the children all shared their birth date of 25th January. The shocking fact becomes that the murder took place on the exact date of their birthdays, which could in turn provide a new and undiscovered motive as to why the children were murdered.

Truthfully, we will never know of what kind of people that Brass family were, but we are so beautiful placed by the narrator in a world where it seemed to look kindly on the family, and everything was running in accordance with God's plan. This however would not last, and in the year 1682, the elder John Brass would have to seek additional hand in the form of an apprentice servant to his farm.

The Murderer

Andrew Mills (or Millns or Miles)

- Baptised: No information available.
- Felon committed: Thursday, 25 January 1683.
- Age at time of murder: Between 18 and 19 years of age. New information suggests he was 17 or 18 years old.
- Date of Birth: No information available. His estimate birth year would be between 1665 and 1666

The person Andrew Mills is as mysterious as the Devil himself. Historians have recorded nothing of his past, his upbringing, how he came into servitude, and none of this information from archives has been shortcoming. He essentially is a shadow in this story.

What little that we do know of Andrew Mills starts in the forbidding year of 1682, when *Jacob Bee*, the aforesaid diarist of Durham, recorded the following statement.

> 'The first day that men and women servants presented themselves to be hired in Durham market was the 6th day of May, 1682.'

To understand the hire of servants in the 17th century, one must refer to the acts of apprenticeships under the Poor Law Act and the Statute of Artificers.

Apprenticeships in England

Apprenticeships in England have its roots back to the 12th Century and were thriving since the 14th. A minimum term of apprenticeship is seven years, but some lasted longer depending on the trade. A person could not enter a trade without serving as an apprentice first.

> 'Persons, having served seven years as apprentices to any trade, have an exclusive right to set up that trade any part of England, except where they are prohibited by the bye-laws or local privileges of divers corporations.
>
> And if a man shall in any town exercise a trade, without served an apprenticeship for seven years, he shall forfeit 40s. a month'

The apprenticeship law in the 16th century mentions how a master or mistress can take on an apprentice, and provides the specific age groups those apprentices must be to serve. This is crucial in relation to Andrew Mills and his master John Brass:

> 'Every person being a house-holder and having and using half a plough-land in tillage, may take an apprentice above the age of ten years and **under eighteen**, to serve in husbandry until twenty-one at the least, or till twenty-four, as the parties can agree',

This means that Andrew Mills would have to be at least 17 years of age at the time of being taken on as an apprentice. The above statement also means that in law, a master is obliged to take on an apprentice if they could not themselves manage to cultivate half their land within one year with only a team of oxen.

The Poor Law Act of 1601

The *Poor Law Act of* 1601, under Queen Elizabeth I, made it the responsibility the each parish, by means of an Overseer of the Poor, to distribute money for the poor by way of taxes and by placing paupers – children of married and unmarried parents had no means to support them – into apprenticeships:

> '...shall be called Overseers of the poor of the same Parish, and they, or the greater part of them shall take order from time to time, by and with the consent of two or more Justices of Peace, as is aforesaid, for setting to work of the children whose parents shall not by the said Churchwardens, and Overseers, or the greater part of them, be thought able to keep and maintain their children. And also for setting to work all such persons married or unmarried, having no means to maintain them, or no ordinary and daily trade of life to get their living by...and also for the putting out of such children to be apprentices'

This means that in one sense, Andrew Mills may not have had parents and could have being a child of the state. It also could mean that if Andrew Mills had a parent or parents, who were either married or not, and those people had no means themselves to support him, that he was forced into apprenticeship by the above Act of the state.

The Statute of Artificers, 1563

The *Statute of Artificers in* 1563 seeked to deter idleness and stop paying any monies which is set above any amounts by law:

> '...should banish idleness, advance husbandry, and yield unto the hired person both in the time of scarcity and in the time of plenty a convenient proportion of wages...'

An agreed term of apprenticeship was placed between both master and servant, unless either shall complain to the authorities of ill treatment, money, etc.:

> '...enacted that no person which shall retain any servant put away his or her servant, and that no person retained according to this statue shall depart from his master, mistress, or dame before the end of his term...unless it be for some reasonable and sufficient cause or matter to be allowed before two justices of peace, or one at the least, within the said county, or before the mayor or other chief officer of the city, borough, or town corporate wherein the said master, mistress, or dame inhabiteth, to whom any parties grieved shall complain; which said justices......shall have take upon them or him the hearing and ordering of the matter between the said master, mistress, or dame, and servant according to the equity of the cause...'

If Andrew Mills did suffer wrong by his master, then he had due right to take his case to the authorities, whereby a hearing between the two parties would be made. The difficulty in 17th Century practice that whilst it is reasonable by law for a servant to prosecute, his/her master or mistress would be able to secure a good solicitor or lawyer to help their case. A servant, by means of money, would simply not be able to do this, unless they can prove by witnesses in court of any illegal activity by his/her master/mistress. Many servants, particularly those of lesser trades such as farming may not have known of the above clause.

The Statute law determines that all apprentices must be indentured, that is to say, to agree and sign a legal document stipulating the exact terms of the apprenticeship.

> 'certify the same, engrossed in parchment with the considerations and causes thereof under their hands and seals, into the Queen's most honourable court of chancery'

Not all of Durham's indentures of labourers and apprenticeships have survived history, and the indenture of Andrew Mills to John Brass in 1682 is part of the missing documents. However even without the missing evidence to support this claim, this way of acceptable employment in the 17th Century is the most likely way of how Andrew Mills became the employee of John Brass at his farm in Ferryhill.

Andrew at the Farm

John Brass's agreement on his apprentice's indenture meant that he must give board and lodgings, and provide woollen and linen clothing, and instruct Andrew in his trade. Andrew must be kept in the same house as his family, and be fed, clothed, and paid accordingly on the condition that this apprentice worked hard.

Andrew Mills as an apprentice must in turn be compliant, productive and organised in his work. He must not attend the theatre for fear of drunkenness – theatres then being close to or in alehouses. Another forcible part of the indenture is that an apprentice must not marry during the time of his/her apprenticeship, for fear for loss of trade and expense. This restriction on marriage may be another motivation for Andrew Mills to exact his revenge on his master and his family, due to John Brass' eldest daughter Jane going to be married at Candlemas.

When Andrew came to Brass Farm, he had hoped that he would serve faithfully and happy with a family, whom he had none. Instead, it is believed that he came into contact with members of the family and their friends who showed prejudice and hate towards him. His only refuge was to seek the comfort of someone whom he could relate to, the young Miss Elizabeth Brass, whom he shared the same mind-set. In the '*Monthly Chronicle of North Country Lore and Legend, Volume One*', (1888), it is said that:

> 'The servant lad, the Andrew Mills aforesaid, was reckoned quiet and inoffensive, and was credited at the same time with deficiency of intellect and a partial derangement of that which he had. Mills and Elizabeth took kindly to each other. She humoured his fancies, and seldom tried to irritate him, as others of the household and casual visitors would sometimes do. Although quiet when let alone, he was wild enough while in anger, and when in this mood, a dangerous light flashed from his usually dull eye.'

John Brass, the young son, in particular hated Mills. John may have seen himself in Mills, as a young man also prone by weakness of character. They were after all of near the same age. However, instead of reckoning with his inner demons, young John saw Andrew Mills, his father's servant, a young man whom his own father became closer than himself, as his target for bullying and nothing was done about it.

> 'The father was blind to his faults – indeed, rather liked them'

Mill's anger was heightened when he felt that others, like John Brass the son, could see his failure. It was only young Elizabeth who could calm him.

> 'But exhibitions of temper was few and far between, and he was never so sullen or so fierce that Elizabeth could not lure him into peacefulness, and engage him in some girlish game'.

Whatever truths or half-truths lies in the series of events of Andrew Mills coming to work for John Brass, nothing it would seem lead to a murder that would be forever spoken of in County Durham for centuries to come.

Chapter 5

'...accidental judgements, casual slaughters,'

Contemporary Evidence 1: 'In the County of Palatine in Durham near Ferry-hill'

PALATINE IN DURHAM, NEAR FERRY-HILL,

Jan. 25th. 1682. Was Acted the most Horrid and Barbarous Murder that ever was heard on in the North or elsewhere, upon the Bodies of John Brasse, Jane Brasse, and Elizabeth Brasse, while their Parents were gone to Ferry-Hill, not half a Mile from their own Home. As may be seen by this following Relation

ON Thursday the 25th of January, 1682. being St. Pauls day, John Brasse and Margaret his Wife, going that Evening to Ferry-Hill (a Town not half a Mile distant from their own House) they left John their Son, Aged Seventeen years; Jane, their daughter about Nineteen years of Age; and Elizabeth, their Daughter, being Ten years of Age. All three were hopeful Children, and well Educated. These three young People being left at Home, with one Andrew Mills their Servant: About Nine of the Clock the same Night, this Andrew Mills came to the House where his Master and Dame were at Ferry-Hill, to Acquaint them with this sad News, saying, Dame, our Johnny and Jeny are both Kill'd. The Mother crying out, Asked what was become of her Little One. This Andrew Mills, Answered and said, there were two Men in the House, whilst he was feeding the Oxen, and he heard one say to the other, Kill All, Kill All. But the Mother Reply'd, Villain, none but thou has Murther'd my Children.

Upon this, People of all Sorts in abundance flocked to the House, (taking the said Andrew Mills along with them) where they found all the three Persons most Barbarously and Inhumanely Murther'd: Their Throats being Cut, their Bodys greatly Mangled, especially their Heads and Necks. Two Axes was found on the Floor all Bloody, both Heads and Handles. This Mills, was suspected by all to be the Murderer, and being searched, found in his Pocket, his Knife all Bloody, but denied the Fact. The Coroner being sent for, and calling a Jury, Impanell'd them; they Examined the Rogue, who denies all. Whereupon the Coroner advising the Jury to withdraw, Examins the Fellow alone, telling him (if he were guilty) and did confess the Fact, he would befriend him in saving his Life. Upon this, the Villain confest he did it, Saying, whilst the two Eldest were asleep (but not in Bed) he Kill'd them both. And afterwards, took the Little one out of its Bed and Murthered that also. He said, after he had so done, he left them all in one Room. In his confession he further saith, he intended but Four dayes before to have Murdred the whole family, but wanted opportunity. What might be the Cause for these Horible Murders, is not yet known, he living there but a short time, and no differences in the Family. Who ever doubts the Truth of this, may be further satisfied by Mr. Samuel Newton at his House in Gray-Friers, whom this Relation was sent to, and does know the Parents of the Murdred-Children, and did know the Children likewise.

LONDON, Printed for T. V. and Sold by Randal Taylor, 1683.

NEWS OF THE DREADFUL MURDER REACHED AS FAR AS LONDON AS CAN BE SEEN CLEARLY AT THE BOTTOM OF THIS COPY OF 1682 [1683] FOLIO SHEET
(COURTESY OF DURHAM CLAYPORT LIBRARY, DURHAM COUNTY COUNCIL)

Date and Persons involved

The Date is Thursday 25th January 1682 (1683). John and his wife Margaret have left their home leaving their children, Jane, John and Elizabeth alone with their servant, Andrew Mills. We are then told that all three children are 'hopeful and educated'.

- If the Brass children are 'hopeful and educated', are we also sensing that Andrew is not?
- Why have the children been left alone?

Terrible News

About 9.00 pm on the same night, Andrew Mills comes to the place where the parents are in Ferryhill, telling Margaret the wife of tragic news, that both 'our Johnny and Jany' are both dead.

- Notice that if Andrew is guilty, why does he come to the house where the parents are to tell them of the murder, instead of running away? Is he actually innocent, or is he trying to claim innocence when guilty?
- Notice that Andrew uses the word 'our', that he does not separate himself from the children, even after they have been murdered.
- Notice also how Andrew uses the children's names, as though his mental stage is lower than that of an 18/19-year-old adolescent.

Margaret then asked 'what has become of her 'Little One' referring to Elizabeth, her youngest daughter. Andrew tells her that whilst he was out of the house, 'feeding the oxen', he sees two men approach the house, and hears one say onto the other 'Kill all, Kill all'. But Margaret, not believing him, condemns him straight off saying 'Villian, none but thou has Murther'd my children!'

- Why does Margaret condemn him so suddenly, is there something of his person – demeanour, clothing, etc – that fails her belief in him, or was it something else? Did Margaret dislike or mistrust Andrew since the day he came to Brass Farm?
- Andrew pleaded innocence for the first time.

The Mob of Ferryhill

Upon hearing the tragic news, the parents and lots of people from the village take the apprehended Andrew Mills back to Brass Farm, where they find the children 'most barbarously and inhumanly murdered: their throats cut and their bodies mangled especially her heads and necks'. Two bloody axes are found on the floor, the heads and handles covered, and whilst Andrew is searched they find a bloodstained knife in his pocket. Andrew pleads his innocence.

- The murder was absolutely ghastly. Could it take only one person to commit such a heinous crime?
- Two axes are found on the floor, suggesting that there were two perpetrators to the crime? Was Andrew Mills right about the two men coming to the house? Or did Andrew use two axes in his killing spree, and if so, why?
- They find a bloodstained knife in his pocket. Who is to say that Andrew may have used the same knife during the course of the day whilst working at the farm? Could Andrew tried to help the children whilst they were been so brutally murdered, by stabbing one of the actual killers, and in the process, become blood-soaked? Perhaps in the stress of the moment, he returned the knife to his pocket whilst he was trying to save the children? Was the knife planted on him whilst he was taken back to Brass farm?
- Andrew claims his innocence the second time.

Innocent or Guilty?

The Coroner is sent for, and upon arrival on the scene, takes a group of people to act as a jury, when he asks Andrew again if he was guilty. Andrew again pleads his innocence.

- Did a coroner have a right to take people who had come to the farm to act as jury people? Surely, his role was to take notes of the murder, and ask the perpetrator if and why he/she did the crime?
- Andrew claims his innocence the third time.

The Coroner, knowing that he is not getting anywhere whilst people are around him, asks everyone to leave the room so he can talk to Andrew alone. When they are alone, he states that Andrew will be befriended if he tells him the truth. At this point, Andrew confesses he was the guilty person.

- Why does Andrew change his plea when left alone with the coroner? Are we so compelled that Andrew needs a friend to confide in to tell the truth?
- Are we to understand that only one person, the coroner, is told of Andrew's guilt when after so long he is claiming innocence?
- Are we to simply trust the coroner's evidence?

How the murders were committed?

The children were murdered in their sleep. The two eldest children were not in bed, suggesting that they were awake and that some commotion had happened with them, and he killed them both. After he was done with them, he took the young child Elizabeth out of her bed, and killed her too. He left them all in one room.

■ This fact of the murders is particularly interesting when we deal with the legendary side of the murders. (Chapter 6)

Andrew said that four days before the awful atrocity, he had intended to murder all of the family, but did not have any opportunity.

■ Not only are we to understand that Andrew Mills of being guilty of triple murders, that there had been in fact premeditation to commit the murder on every member of the Brass family four days prior.

The cause of the murders?

The folio sheet leaves the audience with a final question: Why? Andrew Mills had only lived with the Brass for only a short time, and there had been no differences in the family.

Contemporary Evidence 2: *'The Diary of Jacob Bee'*

The following entry comes from *'The Diary of Jacob Bee'*, living at Durham:

> '1682/3 25 Jan. A sad cruel murther comitted by a Boy about 18 or nineteen years of age, nere Ferryhill, nere Durham, being Thursday at night; The maner is, by report – When the parents were out of dores, a young man, being Sone to ye house, and 2 Daughters, was kil'd by this Boy with an axe, having knockt ym in ye head, afterwards cut their throats, one of ym being asleep in ye bed, about 10 or eleven yeares of age; the other Daughter was to be married at Candlemas. After he had kil'd the Sone and the eldest Daughter, being above twenty yeares of age, a little lass her sister, about ye age of 11 years, he drag'd her out in bed, and killed her alsoe. This Andrew Millns, alias Miles, was hang'd in irons upon a gybett, nere Ferryhill, upon the 15th day of August, being Wednesday, this yeare, 1683.'

It is upon his entry that we learn of Andrew Mills' age at the time of the murders taking place, and Jacob sees Andrew as the guilty person. We learn more of the circumstances of how the murder took place: the parents were away from the house, leaving the children alone with their servant, and exact details of the murder. Again, the historical accounts do not give us the reasons why the atrocity took place, only that Andrew is found guilty and sentenced to be 'hanged in irons upon a gibbet'.

Contemporary Evidence 3: The original grave of the Brass Children

A fragment of the original grave is held within the Church building at Kirk Merrington. In the Cathedral Library in Durham, there is a book by George Allan, called *'Collectanea Dunelmensla'*, and it records the inscriptions as follows:

> 'Here lies the Bodies
> Of JOHN, JANE and ELIZABETH
> Children of
> JOHN and MARGARET BRASS
> who were murther'd by their
> father's servant Jan ye 25th 1682.
>
> Reader rememb'r sleeping
> we were slain,
> & here we sleep till we must
> rise again.
> Whose sheddeth man's blood by
> Man shall his blood be shed
> Thou shall do no murther.'

We are told who was murdered, when the murder took place, and who committed the awful deed. The last part of the inscription reminds us that within law, should man kill another, and then he himself will be killed according to God's Law. The Ten Commandments tells us *'Thou shalt not kill'*.

Whatever remains of the telling of the murder falls into the myths of time and legends.

Chapter 6
'Of deaths put on by cunning, and forc'd cause' – the Lost Hours

The mystery of why the murders took place has haunted local historians for centuries, and it is likely that it will continue to do so. What we are told now falls in into the darkness of legend, when facts merge into folklore. For the helpfulness of the reader, I shall attempt to place you back in time, to witness the event as it unfolds. You have been warned.

The Legend

It had just turned 4.30 pm, and dusk was upon the hill shadowing Brass Farm in a splash of red and orange tones. In the sky, the moon was already out, and was in its first quarter. The house looked unnatural in the setting sun. The air was dense, cold and quiet.

Andrew had just set the horse and cart together so that his master and mistress could visit Ferryhill in order to make the final arrangements for the coming wedding of their elder daughter Jane who has to be married in a week's time. John, his master told Andrew to attend to the oxen before he was to turn in. An apprentice's work never stopped, even though his master was away from his house.

A few hours past whilst Andrew attended to the oxen. The barn was freezing, and dark, and there was only a small candle to light his way. This year's weather had been so dreadful, and Andrew was feeling the pinch, in his mind, his body, and his soul.

As he struggled along, he began to notice that the flame of the candle he held began to shudder violently, as if there was a wind passing through the barn, yet Andrew could not feel anything except for the bitter night cold. Then he began to feel it, an intense cold, colder than he was used to. He noticed too that the barn grew darker, darker than what it usually was, even in the darkest of nights. His gaze returned to the candle flame, which turned blue for a split second and went out. He was alone, scared, and wondering what was next. He then heard two men in the darkness saying *"hear ye, them bairn's all alone."*

"Aye, they are."

"What do thou think? Kill ym?

"Aye, let's kill ym."

"Kill all, kill all, kill all, kill all, kill all."

He tried to penetrate the darkness, to find his way out to investigate who was speaking, and then it dawned on him. The voices were not coming from outside the barn; they were speaking within, and worse, inside him. Andrew tried in vain to ignore them, but his head growled, and the voices growled louder. *"Kill ym, kill ym all. Kill ym. Kill ym all. Kill all. Kill all. Kill ym all!"*

He tried to whistle to control himself and his fears, but the voices continued unabated. At last, he shouted in vain, "No!!! Get thee behind ye, Satan!" and tried to remember the Lord's Prayer. "Our Father, who art in..."

"*Hell.*" One voice finished his sentence.

Andrew stood dead in his tracks. He spoke of Satan and he had replied. He was terrified, but amazed, "Is thou the...?"

"*Devil*", The other voice acknowledged, deeply.

Andrew began to tremble, and his voice broke as he spoke "What does thou want?"

"Thou knows what. Thou master's family has made thou ill. Be not afraid. Do it. Do it. Do it. Kill all. Kill all. Kill all!" the voices commanded.

"Yes", Andrew stared in a daze, a darkness creeping inside him. He left the barn, took two small axes from the wall just outside the barn door, and slowly walked towards the house. In the distance, a dog started howling.

*

The youngest child Elizabeth was asleep, yet the elder siblings Jane and John were still up in the sister's bedroom. The bedroom candles were still ablaze with light. The events of the day had not left them weary, and instead Jane was talking with her brother.

"My dear sister," said John, "I cannot believe that within a week, thou will be married and gone from this place."

"Aye, I will be wed, I am looking forward to the event", replied Jane, "But I will not be far from thee."

"T'is just.... father is getting older, and thou has always helped him with the farm business. Thou are the smart one."

"Thou art too," consoled Jane. "Thou has shown a great interest in our father's work, when thou puts one's mind to it."

"But t'is numbers and stock, and grain and wages. I have no mind to calculate these matters."

"Dear brother, these things are really none important in the grand scheme of things." Jane replied. "T'is love that is important. The rest will simply fall into place. Besides, I will not be far, and still help dear father with these issues, and then when I am with child, we could arrange to hire a man to do undertake the accounts for us."

They both laughed. Jane had always been the smart one in the family, and her wit and humour always calmed the rest of her family down. It was her gift. Her brother John really didn't seem to notice it before, as he was envious of her power, but now he saw it in her, and he was pleased and happy. It would seem at last that everything was glorious and right between them.

Their conversation trailed off when they started hearing noises coming from outside. They both walked to the window, and stared out into the darkness beyond. They could see nothing, but they could hear it. The farm animals were making a commotion and seemed disturbed by something in their midst. A neighbour's dog was howling. In the distance, a nearby church bell began to strike the hour.

"Jane, what be maketh this happen?" John worryingly said to his sister.

"I knoweth not", replied Jane, looking back to her brother, and then starring back to the window.

At that moment, a door banged open from down stairs, and the flames of the bedroom candles began to shudder violently by the sudden cold.

They heard a scraping noise coming up the stairs, followed by a voice, a known voice. "Johnny, Jany, Johnny, Jany. Be thee happy, Be thee merry?" They could hear Andrew's voice coming up the stairs, but it sounded different, mocking and high pitched. "If thou seeth a devil coming, runeth away, thou'd better hurry."

John walking slowly outside the bedroom door, taking a candle with him, his hand trembling and his heart fluttering. "Stay here", he quietly whispered back to Jane in the room. Trying hard to see in the dark passage in front of him, the candlelight caught the steel of a large blade, and the known voice spoke "John, thou will get what thou has done unto me."

Rushing back into the room, John commanded his sister to help him secure the door, as Andrew rushed towards it. They had no time to place anything hard against their side of the room; their bodies were their only hope. Andrew was screaming on the other side, his voice filled with hate.

"Andrew, what has us done onto thou", shouted Jane through the door.

There was no reply. They realised there was no time trying to reason with him, for he would not listen.

Bang! Bang! Bang! Bang!

The sound vibrated though the door onto their shoulders, their bodies, through their souls. They were terrified. Andrew had an axe, and if he could not get passed the door, he would take the door down with him.

Bang! Bang! Bang! Bang!

Elizabeth woke up with a start. Seeing the danger suddenly in front of her, her own dear brother and sister trying to resist the violence behind the bedroom door, she began to sob. Jane spoke quickly, glancing towards her. "Eliza, thou'll be fine as long as we're here." Andrew's voice, the voice that Elizabeth knew all too well, chuckled behind the door.

"He is not yielding. He is possessed!" cried John to his sister. "He must stop soon, the door is strong, and together we are stronger", replied Jane, hoping to give her brother and herself courage.

Bang! Bang! Bang! Bang!
Bang! Bang! Bang! Bang!
Bang! Bang! Bang! Bang!

The constant onslaught to the door worried John, "Andrew!" he screamed though the emerging cracks, "when ye master gets home, thou will not see the morn."

"I think THOU will not", was the automatic reply. "I careth not for my master, and I careth not for THOU." The pounding to the door became stronger.

Bang! Bang! Bang! Bang! Crunch!

"Oh, ye God!" Jane screamed, "ye door's failing. Brother, put all ye strength into it." John and Jane pushed with all their might to keep the door still. The hinges begin to move. "I fear that this be ye end for us", John wailed. Instantly, the door moved inwards, the doorframe was weakened and the hinges had been severed. "OH YE GOD!!!" the pair cried in vain. Jane was suddenly struck with a thought. She moved her left hand out to where the hinges had been, making a makeshift bolt between the door and the doorframe.

One blow of the axe, and the flesh and bones in Jane's arm broke. Jane screamed as the pain shot through her body. In an attempt to bring aid to his sister, John suddenly and without thought moved away from the door, and Andrew broke in, crashing the door down to the floor. He got hold of Jane and sent her flying backwards across the length of the room.

"What hast thou done to my sister!" John screamed. The children had always had their sibling rivalry, but none of them considered physical harm to each other. John managed to stand up away from Jane with remarkable fury in his eyes, his body, and his mouth. "I have always hated thou Johnny, but this time, there be no more taunting of me." The act of violence against his own flesh and blood was enough to claim physical assault against a man who had dared to harm one of them.

John was on Andrew like a flash, kicking, punching, biting, scraping, and ensuring any sort of harm that would put the mad man down. However, years of doing odd jobs and working on the farm had made Andrew stronger than John had wished for, and so, Andrew fought back, and John was knocked cold by the steady blow of his hand. John hit the floor hard. His head hurt, the room was spinning and he felt sick. He tried to glance up. The last thing that John attempted to see was Andrew bringing up his arms backwards; see the glint of something metallic, and the bringing down of the axe upon the top of his head.

Clunk. Jane and Elizabeth screamed.

Jane tried to move herself across the floor towards her dear brother but her hand and body failed her. She was in too much pain. "Andrew, thou's a monster!" she screamed up at him. Andrew came towards her, bent down, grabbed her by her neck, and pushed her head against the wall. With his other hand, he went to his pocket, and brought out a small knife. He flicked the blade towards her. "A monster?" he sneered. "Thou have more love than they care to share, more love than me. I, who can never marry while in servitude, whilst thou flaunt yourself in the town. Thou should be ashamed." He smiled. "Thou will never marry like I." With this, as his left hand was pressed against her, his other hand struck the blade in tight.

Jane's body withered and contorted on the floor. Andrew pulled the knife out. Blood splurged out of the neck wound. Jane finally stopped moving. Andrew placed the knife back into his pocket, a trophy.

Elizabeth who sat on her bed the whole time was too shocked and too scared to move, let alone speak. She knew that if she had moved or spoken out in his wild temper, she would suffer.

Andrew stood up from Jane's body, breathing heavily. He dazed down on the bodies of the brother and sister, his face twisted. They deserved it, he thought. Minutes passed and Andrew was still starring down upon them. Elizabeth dared not move, but a rustle of her bed sheets woke Andrew from his daze. He came towards her, and went for her hair, pushing and pulling her head like a rag doll.

"Andrew, please let me be," sobbed the little girl. "Thou art my friend. I have never harmed thou." Some humanly feeling returned to Mills, and he let go of her. Elizabeth continued. "I will give thou everything of mine. My toys, my father's sugar, bread or butter from the larder. Anything thou wish."

"Thank thee", replied Andrew. "I will not harm thee, I promise." He moved away from Elizabeth, and walked out of the bedroom. "I'll leave here, never t'return." Elizabeth was still on her bed, afraid to run.

"TRAITOR!" a fearful voice screamed. He looked back at Elizabeth but he knew it was not she. It was the same voice he heard earlier. He went to the passage to look. In the dark, he saw a hideous creature that could only have visited him in his worst nightmares. His mouth flung open. A beast of a creature, It's head was the shape of a wolf, the eyes a fiery red. The body resembled that on an eagle, and was lifted by two misshapen stag-like legs. The most prominent feature was its enormous wings that took the whole space of the hallway. It spoke with an unchristian croak.

"Oh, ye God", Andrew whimpered.

"Andrew, thou a traitor to me. Thou master's family hast given you nothing, yet you leave this thing be", screamed the beast.

"The thing thou say is my friend", replied Andrew.

"Thou hast no friends. I WARNED THOU."

"Please no...." Andrew stood, his glaze transfixed to the glowing fiery eyes in front of him.

The thing began to chant. "*Go back thou hateful WRETCH. Resume thy cursed KNIFE. I long to view more BLOOD. Spare not the young one's LIFE. Kill all, Kill all, Kill all, Kill all, Kill all, Kill all, Kill all, Kill all, Kill all, Kill all, Kill all*"

The relenting of the voice would not stop. Andrew tried desperately to put his hands over his ears, but he could still hear the ghastly words.

"Aaaahhhhhhhhhhh," he screamed. Picking up his axe, he returned to the room where Elizabeth remained. She was not on her bed. He glanced round the room, fuming. The flickering candle caught the shadow of the young girl's hand. Of course, she had moved under it.

"Where art thou, Lizzy?" He mocked, swinging the axe back and forth.

His feet reached the bedpost. "GET YE OUT OF BED!" Andrew bellowed down to the mattress. There was no reply. "IF THOU WILT NOT, I WILL!" Andrew knelt down, grabbed the girl by her leg, and pushed her out of the bed towards him.

"Andrew, please", screamed the girl looking up at him.

"Shut thou up!" returned Andrew. Elizabeth placed her hands on the top of her head, as Andrew once again brought the cold wood up, and then the hard steel down.

"Andrew, ple---"

"Rraaaawwwwwhhhhhh!!!!!!!"

Clunk.

Clunk.

Clunk.

Clunk.

Clunk.

Finally, Andrew stopped, the end of the axe pointed to the floor, but the handle still remained tight in his hand. It would seem that the fire within him was gone. He looked around him. The room and its occupants were a figureless, frightful mess. No words could describe what he had done.

He looked to his once young friend; her brains were splattered from her. She did not move. Nothing inside him moved him emotionally to the once happy times he had shared with her. He neither smiled nor frowned. Nothing.

He glanced towards the elder children. "Jany, ye most beautiful women I have ever met, yet ye flaunted thyself in front of me with another man'. The heat built up. "How dareth thou?" he thought. He turned in disgust to John. "Thou were a BASTARD TO ME!" he screamed down to the thing below, its wild eyes staring back at him, unmoving.

Andrew thought he heard the return of the brother's voice. "Thou's the bastard, Andrew", the open eyes mocking said back. With this final remark, whether Andrew had just heard it or it was from the failing corpse, he was not sure, but it created another huge spark inside him, and he brought the axe up and down to finish his tormentor's life.

Clunk. Chunk. Clunk.
Clunk. Chunk. Clunk.
Clunk. Chunk. Clunk.
Clunk. Chunk. Clunk.
Clunk. Chunk. Clunk.
Clunk. Chunk. Clunk.

He looked at the other bodies. He was sure that they too were dead, but the faces seemed alive. The problem was that these faces were not those he knew when they were alive, but faces of demons, laughing at him, mocking him...

He went round the room with the knife and axe, pushing the blades up and down, up and down, up and down in their faces, numerous times until the demons were no more.

Clunk. Chunk. Stab... Stab...
Clunk. Chunk. Stab... Stab...
Clunk. Chunk. Stab... Stab...
Clunk. Chunk. Stab... Stab...
Clunk. Chunk. Stab... Stab...
Clunk. Chunk. Stab... Stab...
Clunk. Chunk. Stab... Stab...

He began to feel ill; the smell of blood was upon him and around him. He dropped the axe, crashing it to the floor. He unconsciously put the knife back in his trousers. The blades and handles were sticky red. He looked like he had worked in a slaughterhouse or a butcher's shop.

The last thing he remembered was him running though the passage, down the stairs, springing out of the front door, and screaming, screaming, screaming, to the ready, consuming darkness of the world outside.

Other Stories

Some stories have the parents, John and Margaret Brass, returning home on their horse and cart, when suddenly dogs in nearby fields began to howl, and the horse freezes on the dirt road, John unable to bug it. Out in the darkness, movement on the road ahead could be heard, and out of the darkness, Andrew emerges; his eyes wild, yet he speaks not a word, and hurry passes them. John and Margaret know something is terribly wrong, gets the horse to move again, and with all haste, get to the house where they discover the dead children. In the meantime, Andrew is captured by some troops that were heading to Durham from Darlington the very night.

Another story has Andrew coming to the house where John and Margaret were on the night of the murders, telling them of the dreadful news. The landlady, seeing the blood of his person, sprang upon him, stating, "Andrew, thou's the man."

No contemporary sources have ever been found to back up any of the events in this chapter. Perhaps it is for the best that the exact details of the murder remain unsolved: it would escape the reader of how the children lost their lives and give us hope that they were indeed asleep when they were so brutally killed. That being said, it would settle the final details of *'the most horrid and barbarous murder that was ever heard in the North or elsewhere.'*

Chapter 7
The Missing Evidence

Robert Surtees of Mainsforth in County Durham, the famous northern historian in the 19th Century, wrote in his book '*The History and Antiquities of the County Palatine of Durham, Volume 3*' (1823):

> 'According to the murderer's own confession (*and on this point no other evidence could be had*), neither provocation nor cause of quarrel had arisen; and he persisted to the last in stating, that he had acted on an immediate suggestion of *the enemy* (who according to some accounts appeared to him *bodily*)'

It is not therefore surprising that for over 300 years since the murders took place, no further contemporary evidence has come to light to give the final details of the murders and why he did it.

Copies of coroner's report still exist in the National Archives, however there is an 11-year gap in the records, between 1674/5 (*DURH* 17/1/16) and 1686 (*DURH* 17/1/17).

The indictment (court sentence) rolls of the North and North Eastern Assize Court (*ASSI* 44/31) of 1683 are still available but most of the court rolls of the 17th century is in Latin.

Part Three

'How came he dead?

Chapter 8

'Let come what comes: only I'll be reveng'd'

Burial of the Brass Children

The day after the murders, on Friday 26th January 1683, the bodies of the Brass children were placed within white linen then transported slowly by horse and cart, with their mother, father, and a procession of other people behind them, to the churchyard of Kirk Merrington. Vicar Thomas Knaggs, who was posted to the church only the year before, attended to their burial service:

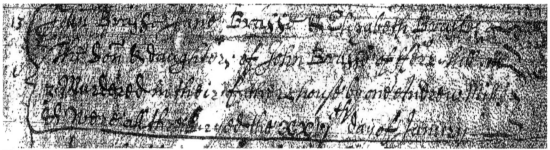

THE BURIAL RECORD OF THE SON AND DAUGHTERS OF JOHN BRASS OF FERRYHILL. (DRO EP/MER 2).
(PROVIDED BY COURTESY OF DURHAM RECORD OFFICE AND THE INCUMBENT PARISH OF MERRINGTON)

'13. John Brass, Jane Brass, & Elizabeth Brass
The Son & Daughters of John Brass of Ferryhill, all
3 murdered in their father's house by one Andrew Mills,
& were all three buryed the xxvith day of January'

Their tombstone, a simply stone laid flat on the ground, gave the following inscription:

'Here lies the Bodies
Of JOHN, JANE and ELIZABETH
Children of
JOHN and MARGARET BRASS
who were murther'd by their
father's servant Jan ye 25th 1682.

Reader rememb'r sleeping
we were slain
& here we sleep till we must
rise again
Whose sheddeth man's blood by
Man shall his blood be shed
Thou shall do no murther.'

It is assumed that John and Margaret Brass and anyone who knew and respected the family paid handsomely for the children's burial, no doubt from the money that was due to Jane, their eldest daughter, upon her marriage that never happened.

THE SITE OF DURHAM GOAL, IN SADDLER STREET DURHAM CITY, NOW A SIMPLE ROAD LEADING UP THE CATHEDRAL (AUTHOR'S PHOTOGRAPH)

Goal imprisonment of Andrew Mills

Andrew Mills, on the same day, was transported into Durham City Goal at Saddler Street and await the next assizes to be tried for the children's murders.

Durham was the centre point of dealing with criminals and felonies for the county. The Quarter sessions dealt with petty crime such as theft. The Assizes court however, which only happened maybe once or twice a year, dealt with major crime. A book dated 1654, called '*An ordinance for enabling the Judges or Judges of the Northern Circuit, to hold Assizes and Goal Deliveries in Durham*', mentions that:

> 'And that further Process, Proceeding, Trial, Judgement and Execution, may be had thereupon, as in other Counties, upon the like Writs, Process and Actions. And that they the aforesaid Justice, or Justices, be assigned, shall likewise hear and determine all, and all manner of Treasons, Petty Treasons, Murders, Manslaughters, Felonies, Burglaries, Rapes, Riots, Routs, Unlawful Assemblies, and all other offences and injuries, triable, done or committed by any persons whatsoever, within the said Countie of Durham, against any statutes or Laws of this Nation...and also from time to time to make or cause to be made Delivery and Deliveries at the Goal of the said County, according to the Law....and that the said Justice or Justices shall act, do and perform the said matters and things, in such manner and form, as any other Justice or Justices of Assizes, or other Justice of the Peace of the Crown, Common Pleas, at other pleas at Durham...'

The conditions of the Goal cells were terrible. Placed in a room less than 6 feet in length by 10 feet in width, the height being approximately 8 meters, the person in jail had to content with wearing the same clothes as he or she wore on the date of their crime, as a reminder of what they did. The walls and the floor of the cell were dirty and damp. The room was freezing. A patch of hay with an old ragged sheet on top was their bed. Food was inadequate. The prisoner was perhaps given meals three or four times a week: an undercooked potato and a bit of stale bread, and some water in a jug to swill it down, if they were lucky. Their companions would have been the rats that ran in and out the cells, collecting the untouched, uncooked foods that the prisoner left behind. There was no light in the room, except for the candles that flickered on the corridor outside, or if they were privileged with a barred window, they would see the outline of the cathedral above and pray to God for their shortcomings. There was little to no communication from the outside world.

Andrew Mills remained in these conditions from the 26th January to the 4th of August 1683, a period of 6 months, and eight days, when the next assize court began. An entry in 'The Diary of Jacob Bee' tells us that:

> '1683. 3 Aug. The assizes began, and such an inundation of watter [water] that the judges was forcet to come down Gillygate [Gilesgate] and come in about 8 at night, and read their commission. Judges names, Jones and Strut.'

The Assize Court was at the top of Saddler Street, outside Durham Cathedral, at Palace Green, which is now the building of the Durham University Archives and Special Collections.

THE POSSIBLE SITE OF THE ASSIZE COURT AT DURHAM, NOW THE HOME OF DURHAM UNIVERSITY ARCHIVES AND SPECIAL COLLECTIONS (AUTHOR'S PHOTOGRAPH)

Historians have never pointed to the exact dates of Andrew Mill's trial at the assize court but one could estimate the dates being between the 4th and the 14th August of that year.

The trial was preceded over by members of the King's Bench, either by Sir Thomas Jones (Judge from 1676 to 1686) or Thomas Street (Judge from 1677 to 1689). Perhaps the months of isolation had made Andrew Mills more seriously ill in his mind, or perhaps his mind, to him at least, was clearer about the events of 25th January, but it would be here that Andrew Mills or his defence, could he afford one, would have mentioned that his actions on the night of the murders were simply influenced by the Devil.

Chapter 9
'To hell allegiance: vows, to the blackest devil...'

The Devil

When Andrew Mills approached the court bench to give his confession for what happened on the night of the murders, he had stated that no provocation occurred, and his actions were the result of being suggested by the Devil. William Longstaffe, author of *'The History and Antiquities of the Parish of Darlington'* (1854), mentions that:

> 'Tradition adds that the wretch's intention as to the youngest child was half frustrated by her entreaties and promises of bread, butter, and sugar, and some toys, but that of going of the room he met in the passage a hideous creature like a fierce wolf with red fiery eyes, its two legs were like those of a stag, its body resembled an eagle, and was supplied with two enormous wings; this apparition addressed Mills with a most unchristian croak with the words:
>
> *Go back, thou hateful wretch, resume thy cursed knife,*
> *I long to view more blood, spare not the young one's life.*
>
> And the injunction was obeyed.'

Once again, we are reminded in the old texts that Andrew had a mind of a child inside the body of an 18-year-old. He was fond of a 'sugar sandwich' and toys. The very essence of child-like things had stopped him in his tracks and might have saved the youngest child from the evil of the night had the Devil not visited him in bodily form.

In the 17th century, it was no distinction between acts caused by the Devil and acts caused by mental illness. Mental illness in its own right was not even thought of until the 19th century.

According to pamphlets and printed books of the time, the Devil was the cause of man's many faults, for it is he that according to the Bible, tempted the first human beings to eat from the tree in the Garden of Eden, to tempt Jesus in the Judean Dessert, and again at the mount of Jerusalem. The Devil was the enemy of man, and it was in man's best interest to ensure that he was prepared for the daily evil of the world around him.

Demonic Oppression

The act of demonic oppression is believed to be where devils or demons reduce the human body and mind to such an extent that the person is devoid of life, can be tempted into sin, to deny God's Word, and to feel absolutely spiritually closed off. Any person, even Christians, can be harmed through demonic oppression when their belief in God is low, if their mind is not strong, or open themselves to events, places, or people where there is strong satanic or paranormal influence.

The symptoms or effects of demonic oppression can be constant sleeplessness or tiredness; abnormal nightmares; anxiety; thoughts of self-harm or harm to others; addictions;

hallucinations; physical illnesses; sudden anger where there is no provocation; cold or unblinking eyes; scratches or marks on the body with no determinable way of cause; depression; hyperactivity; acute awareness; self-validation; constant fear or hopelessness; abnormal fixations; delusions, constant apathy; hatred towards anything holy; and interests in unholy systems or beliefs.

We know from 19th century local historians, that Andrew Mills was initially thought of as being of low intellect and partially deranged.

> 'The servant lad, the Andrew Mills aforesaid, was reckoned quiet and inoffensive, and was credited at the same time with deficiency of intellect and a partial derangement of that which he had'

Such mind-set would allow demons to manifest in such a way to cause demonic oppression. We are led to understand that Andrew showed no provocation to murder, except when he was tormented by others, he would become extremely angry:

> 'Although quiet when let alone, he was wild enough while in anger, and when in this mood, a dangerous light flashed from his usually dull eye.'

We know also that Andrew had a desire to murder all of the Brass family four days prior to the actual murder of the children, but did not have opportunity.

Demonic oppression can eventually prepare the human for demonic possession.

Demonic Possession

Demonic Possession is a force where the human being has limited or no control of his mind or body whatsoever, and it is the devil or demons that have the power. Although the devil and his demons show no regard for God, they do fear Him, so only an ordained priest can perform an exorcism on a person believed to be oppressed or possessed.

It is debatable whether Christians or any other religious sects can be demonically possessed, but they can be oppressed.

The symptoms or effects of demonic possession range from mild to severe, and these are believed to be: blackouts; no control over words said or gestures made; scratches or marks on the body with no determinable way of cause; incredible and unjust anger; speaking in a foreign tongue when no knowledge of the language has been previously learned; speaking gibberish; hysterical laughter; knowledge of the future; knowledge of people's past events or family history where no former contact or knowledge with/of the other person has been made; absolute hatred, aversion, and mocking of all things holy; and extra sensory perception. The severe symptoms or effects of demonic possession are: seen/evidenced levitation; poltergeist activity (e.g. the power to move or throw items or objects without touching them); inhuman / super strength; power to shift the body into unnatural postures; and manifestations of spirits on and around the human body.

Demonic possession also involves a horrid smell, like the smell of sulphur.

It is uncertain whether Andrew Mills would have classified as demonically possessed on the night of the murders, but we are fully aware that, according to 19th century historians, he is the only person responsible for the murder of three people, that there was no provocation; that he had shown some higher strength to break Jane's arm and break down the bedroom door, and to create a 'horrid and barbarous' massacre.

Schizophrenia

As the human population moved onwards to the 19th and 20th centuries, we could no longer blame everything on the Devil and his dominions, because our superstitious attitudes towards the Devil faded and our research into mental health and the human mind became more prominent. The symptoms of demonic oppression and possession can easily be classified as mild to severe schizophrenia.

According to *Schizophrenia.com*, a person with this sad mental illness will show some, if not all, of the following symptoms:

- Paranoid delusions, and allusions;
- Hallucinations;
- Disorganised or poverty of speech;
- Lack of Emotion and facial expression;
- Catatonic behaviour, or extreme flexibility;
- Lack of self-care;
- Lack of memory of thought processes;
- Unable to express or read feelings.

The average onset of schizophrenia mostly starts in men from the age of 16 to 25, whilst women with the condition starts around age 25 to 30. Andrew Mills falls right into the target age group, as he was aged 18-19 at the time when the murders took place.

A lot of people consider those to have schizophrenia to show violent behaviour, however cases are rare, but do exist.

We are reminded that Andrew Mills heard voices commanding him to murder the family, and he saw the devil in the upstairs hallway after murdering the two elder children and returning to murder the third after being commanded again. We also know that according to the folio sheet of 1682, that he used a simple wording for '*Jany*' and '*Johnny*' as a reference to Jane and John the children.

Conclusion

In the 17th century, there was no prescribed medication for treatment of mental disorders. Any treatments would be through local herbal remedies, and these too were not efficient enough to slow down mental disorder, and could in fact bring forth the medical condition faster, if any hallucigenic plants were used.

It is also important to state that we are provided of Andrew Mills' personality 150 years after the murderous event took place, and there is no real contemporary evidence that Andrew Mills did suffer from any mental illness, apart from the two references: the first being the use of child-like words when talking of the death of the elder children Jane ('*Jany*') and John ('*Johnny*'), and the second being his repetitive lying (or repetitive truth).

If Andrew Mills did not suffer from any mental disorder, or was not demonically oppressed or possessed, could there be another reason or motive for murder?

Chapter 10

'Conscience and grace, to the profoundest pit.'

Jealousy

Marriage

Once again, we must return to *'The Diary of Jacob Bee'* who in 1683, records the following:

'...the other Daughter was to be married at Candlemas.'

Could the idea of Jane being married to another man, or the rejection of love from Jane spark the murderous intentions of the night of January 25th? We know that as part of Andrew Mills' apprenticeship to John Brass, he would not be able to marry until after his term with his master was over.

Robert Surtees, in his book *'The History and Antiquities of the County Palatine of Durham: Volume 3'*, (1823), mentions the possibility of jealousy of Jane's marriage:

'Is it not, however, possible, that *jealousy* had some share in producing the horrible catastrophe? Andrew Mills was, it seems, alone with the eldest girl, "who was to be married at Candlemas;" and during his nocturnal conference, might not his sleeping passions, have been roused into madness by some rejection or disappointment?'

Many historians have stuck to his premise, but could there be another motive, hidden throughout history, that would play close to the truth?

Birthdays

Let us consider a new motive for murder, one that has never been known, and is based on the assumption that the all children did share the same birthday date, and they were murdered on the same day.

It is proposed that Andrew Mills comes from a poor background, and neither any of his parents or carers, prior to him becoming an apprentice, share in his birthday, or any other significant event of his life that would be special to him? Let us suppose that in 1682, Andrew Mills is indentured as an apprentice to John Brass during his 17th year, but reaches his 18th birthday between August 1682 and January 1683. Whilst working as a servant for John Brass, no one from the family shows the slightest bit of interest in him.

Let us consider that on 21st January 1683, four days prior to murders, he sees presents for the children's birthdays enter the house. Imagine Andrew seething on this, of how all of the children are been spoilt, and that no one has ever bothered about him? We are led to believe, from 19th century historians, that Andrew Mills had a mind of a child. Would it be possible that form of jealousy, towards a family who he knew he had to share another 6 and a half years before the end of his apprenticeship would never share a single bit of happiness with him, and at a society where the poor remained poor, and the adequately wealthy remained wealthy and had shown no respect to him and his kind. This alone could have made him want to hurt the family in a form of a revenge attack?

We now know that the children of John and Margaret Brass shared the same birth date of 25th January, and that all three were murdered on the night of their birthdays? Would this be the whole reason for their demise?

No Motive

Innocence

Perhaps Andrew Mills was telling the truth all along, that he witnessed two men approach the house, one saying to the other, '*Kill all. Kill all*'. Are we simply going to put this down as a hallucination, or did it actually happen?

We are reminded that two blood stained axes were found on the floor, suggesting that there were two perpetrators to the murders, not one. We are also reminded that Andrew Mills did not run away but in fact came to the house where the parents were at, informing them of their children's murders.

■ Could Andrew Mills have used his pocket knife as a form of defence?

■ Was Andrew Mills himself become a victim of circumstance, that as he was the only one left in the house when the parents left, that he is the sole person responsible for the murders?

■ Was his confession false and was his trial based on circumstantial evidence only?

We will never know why Andrew Mills murdered as he did…if he did…

Chapter II
'I dare damnation: to this point I stand.'

The Death Sentence on Andrew Mills (13 to 14 August 1683)

Hanged in Durham

'Andrew Mills, thou hast been found guilty to a peer of this realm to be the sole executor of a horrid and barbarous act in the county palatine of Durham, on said night of January 25th, 1682, where thou, coldly and without mercy, murthered the said children of thou master, John Brass of the township of Ferry-hill, in thy care. For this act, and this act alone, this court sentences thou to death. Thou will go from this place hence; to be hang'd by the neck to thou be dead. Thou body will be then taken to the place of your heinous act, and cast into irons and hanged upon a gybett to warden off all evil doers, to n'ver again carry out such an unnecessary tragedy'

No record of the death sentence on Andrew Mills has ever been found. The above statement is simply a fabrication of a speech that would have been a fact of reality of the time. Whatever the reason why Andrew murdered the children will never be truly known, but the court sentenced him to his death.

Andrew would have been placed in a wooden cart, and escorted out of Durham, to be taken to his place of execution. Durham City would have packed, as people always do, when they want to watch a display. Some people would have come to find out more of the young man responsible for the crime of murder, some people came to watch justice being done, and some people came to satisfy their own sick mentality, to watch another human being been hung. Andrew would have had to suffer the crowd, their abuses, and people throwing rotten fruit and vegetables at him. People tried to have their own satisfaction, by trying to get close to the prisoner and attempt to stab him, only to be pushed away by the soldiers.

There is no worse sin than being totally cut off by God and humanity by your own hand.

There are three possible locations for public executions on the outskirts of Durham: the first being the now playing field of St Leonard School near County Hall; the second being Black Western Hill; and the third being Dryburn, at the present location of the University Hospital of North Durham, where most public executions took place until 1816. Legend has it that a Jesuit present was hanged at Dryburn, and the local stream (burn) dried up completely, hence the place name. The most likely scenario was that the place was named after other areas of execution, such as Tyburn, in Middlesex.

The cart that Andrew Mills was bound was placed under a triangular post, a gallows, consisting of three virtual wooden pillars, and at the top of the pillars ran a wooden beam adjoining each other, where the execution ropes was fastened. The prisoner would watch and listen to the shouts of abuse and taunts from the angry crowd,

"Kill him!"

"Murderer!"

"Devil!"

Some prisoners even retaliated back, hissing, spitting and swearing back at the crowd; some prisoners spoke of their innocence or guilt, sometimes reading their confession, or put their bound hands up to the heavens and asking for forgiveness. Meanwhile they are told or moved to stand up, and the ligature of the end of the rope is placed tightly around his neck. The last thing would be his own heart bounding in his chest as the last reminder of why life is sacred.

A moment later, the horse carrying the cart was jolted away and the prisoner's body swung violently off the ground, his body twitching and turning whilst the rope cut off the circulation to his brain, his heart and his lungs.

A few minutes later, the body of Andrew Mills fell still. He was dead.

One would have hoped that this would be the end of justice for the murders, but 17th century capital punishment dictated that any persons guilty of murder would be hung first, and then his body placed in an iron cage and took back to the scene of their crime, to be showcased upon a 'gibbet' to stop further offences.

In '*Antient Funeral Monuments, of Great-Britain, Ireland, and the islands adjacent*' by John Weever (1631), we are told:

> 'He who commits the crying sin of murder, is usually hanged up in chains, so to continue until his body be consumed, at, or near the place where the fact was perpetrated'

In '*Angliae Notitia: or, The Present State of England: the First Part*' (1676) it is mentioned that:

> '...as for Murdering and Robbing, any person, then by Order is the Criminal usually hanged by the neck, till he be dead, and afterwards hanged in Chains till the Body rot...'

In '*Certain Sermons or Homilies Appointed to be Read in Churches In the Time of Queen Elizabeth of Famous Memory: and now Reprinted for the use of Private Families*' (1687), it mentioned how a person's dishonour to God would be should they commit such as heinous act:

> 'But commonly they be rewarded with shameful Deaths, their Hands and Carcasses set upon poles, and hanged in Chains, eaten with Kites and Crows, judged unworthy the honour of Burial; and so their Souls, if they repent not, (and commonly they do not), the Devil hurrieth them into Hell in the midst of their mischief.'

In '*The New State of England Under their Majesties K. William and Q. Mary*' (1693), the following is recorded:

> 'As for Persons found guilty of Murder, Theft, or Robbery, and other Capital Crimes, they are (as before said) conducted in a Cart to the Place of Execution, and there hanged, till they be dead. And, when the Robbery is attended with Murder, the Criminal, after he is hanged and dead, is taken down to be hanged in chains, and so to hang in terrorem, till the Body be quite rotted off, or eaten up by the Birds of the Air'

In 1752, a new Murder Act was passed, and it is here, for the first time in British Law, that the process of persons been *'hung in chains'* was recognised:

'...all persons who shall be found guilty of wilful murder, be executed according to law, on the day next but one after sentence passed, unless the same shall happen to be the Lord's day, commonly called Sunday, and in that case on the Monday following:'

'II. And be it further enacted ...that sentence shall be pronounced in open court immediately after the conviction of such murderer...'

'...V. Provided also, That it shall be in the power of any judge or justice to appoint the body of any such criminal to be hung in chains: but in no case whatsoever shall be suffered to be buried, unless after such body shall be dissected and anatomised as aforesaid'.

Hanged in Chains (15 August 1683)

The Gibbet at Ferryhill

'This Andrew Millns, alias Miles, was hang'd in irons upon a gybett, nere Ferryhill, upon the 15th day of August, being Wednesday, this yeare, 1683.'
(Jacob Bee Diary, 1683)

The body of Andrew Mills remained hung on the gallows for a day, as was the usual practice, and then afterwards cut down, his body covered in tar to preserve his body, and then placed in an iron cage, made by a blacksmith to the prisoner's height and weight. He was then taken back to the scene of his crime on Wednesday 15th August 1683, to a site a mile north of Ferryhill, between the said town and Thinford, by the roadside, and the iron cage was hung on a wooden post called a gibbet.

AN EXAMPLE OF AN EXISTING GIBBET BY THE ROADSIDE – WINTER'S GIBBET IN NORTHUMBERLAND
(COURTESY OF GRAEME PATTISON @NEWCASTLEMALE.DEVIANTART.COM)

At the foot of the post would have been inscribed with something of this nature:

A.M.
1683

Legend has it that Andrew Mills survived his execution by hanging or was not executed at all, but instead survived for a period of several days on the gibbet in his iron cage, and was fed by milk by his sweetheart. A 'penny loaf' was placed on an iron spike in front of his face, so when he attempted to eat it, the spike would enter his throat, causing him pain. His moans and cries brought misery to the neighbourhood, and many people left their homes until his agonising were heard no more. It is said that he *'expired with a shriek that was heard from miles around'*.

When we examine closer at the facts though, there has never been any sort of judicial process where a murderer was suffered to live in his iron cage on a gibbet. If this would be true, then the law would be as guilty of murder as the murderer they would condemn. On a more logical approach, the post of the gibbet would have been at least 12 to 15 feet high, making it impossible, except by ladder, to reach the iron cage where it was hung. Albert Hartshorne, in his book *'Hanging in Chains'* (1891), makes the case quite clear:

> 'Similarly, we have a story from Durham, showing that one Andrew Mills, gibbeted alive in 1684 for murdering his master's three children, was kept in existence for some time by his sweetheart (of course), who, until she was prevented, gave him milk in a sponge at the end of a stick.
>
> These kind of stories usually fall to pieces when they are examined, and it so happens that the tombstone of the three unfortunate little children, in Merrington churchyard, are the words: - "He was executed and afterwards hung in chains"; but "executed and" have been nearly obliterated by deep chisel marks, thus forming at once both the *post hoc* and *propter hoc* of the story. As for the milk, and the sweetheart, this part of the fable is nothing but a free rendering'

The facts are clear: Andrew Mills was hung by rope in Durham, and afterwards brought to Ferryhill and cast onto a gibbet.

His corpse at Thinford Crossroads

No record remains of his burial. We are reminded that those guilty of murder are *'judged unworthy the honour of Burial'* so a more likely conclusion would be that after a certain time, his body would be taken out of the gibbet, and burned or buried at a local crossroads. The closest crossroads was at Thinford.

It is believed that crossroads were places of unusual dread, especially at night. Since pagan times, crossroads (an area where two roads join and pass over each other, creating a four road system) were believed to be where the physical world and spiritual world was close to each other, thereby it was easier for ghosts, spirits, vampires, demons and even the Devil were able to manifest.

If one put places like crossroads into a religious context, one could easily link it to the cross of which Jesus Christ was crucified on. Jesus was placed in the centre of cross. If it so happens that spirits are able to manifest more easily at crossroads, they would be bound to the centre. Legends have it that because it is a four lane system, the spirit would be confused as to which direction to take, and so be left standing in the centre until the sunrise, but it would be woe to the lonely traveller who at night coming to the crossroads, and experience a ghostly encounter.

It is also the fact that people who committed suicide, or as it was then called self-murder, were buried at crossroads, as the church would not allow burial in sacred ground. Their heads would be smashed in, and an iron stake was plunged through their body into the bottom part of the coffin, binding them inside so their souls would not escape and torment the living. This same idea gives rise to superstitious creatures, such as vampires and vengeful ghosts. Criminals hanged on gallows that were placed at the crossroads, like Tyburn, were buried in the ground under same the rope that ended their lives.

Chapter 12
'That both the worlds I give to negligence'

'Cutty Throat Farm'

After the murders, locals gave Brass House a terrible nickname – 'Cutty Throat Farm'. The location will always be renowned for a place of murder, which still has an impact on the community to this very day.

John and Margaret Brass never moved away from Ferryhill. In the 17th century, tenants of the Dean and Chapter of Durham didn't have much opportunity to move home and so they spent the rest of their lives in the same house where their children once lived and were murdered in cold blood.

Death of Margaret Brass, 1703

Nothing is known of Margaret Brass' life after the murders. As we are not sure if she had an extended family to additionally support her, she may have spent the rest of her life in deep depression supported only by her husband, wondering if they had remained at home on the terrible evening of January 25th, 1683, would have it made a difference in the saving of their children's lives? Perhaps this idea put a massive strain on their marriage? We simply don't know.

All we know is that 15 years after the tragic event, Margaret passed away just before Christmas. The Register of Merrington records her death in 1703.

THE BURIAL OF MARGARET BRASS, IN THE PARISH REGISTER OF MERRINGTON (DRO EP/MER 2)
(COURTESY OF DURHAM COUNTY RECORD OFFICE AND THE INCUMBENT PARISH OF MERRINGTON)

'[1703] Margaret the wife of John Brass
of Ferry Hill, Buried December 16th'

Her grave, next to her children's, once gave the following inscription and may give a clue as to her physical or mental state, or even her marriage just before passing away.

'1703. Margaret Brass, Wife of John Brass.
In Peace Therefore Lie Down Will I
Taking My Rest and Sleep,
For Thou only Wilt Me, O, Lord
Alone in Safety Keep.
Dun By Me, A. Kay'

John Brass seemed to be of stronger in character than that of his wife, Margaret

John Brass became connected to the church. In 1690, 1693, and again in 1713, he became a churchwarden for Ferryhill, in the Parish of Merrington. The parish minister or vicar usually chose churchwardens annually. The chosen churchwardens' role was to superintend the church, its property, and its concerns.

Churchwarden

PARISH OF MERRINGTON – CHURCHWARDEN AND VESTRY ACCOUNTS, 1690 (DRO EP/MER 34)
(COURTESY OF DURHAM COUNTY RECORD OFFICE AND THE INCUMBENT PARISH OF MERRINGTON)

'Church-wardens chosen on ye year 1690.
Merrington – Ralph Rawling
Ferry-hill – John Brass
Chilton – Ruth? Bruck
Hett – John Adamson'

In 1693, he is recorded in the Merrington Parish vestry and account book, as paying a plumber by the name of 'Henry Richardson of ye old bailey in Durham' for repaint the 'seeds' in the parish church:

PARISH OF MERRINGTON – CHURCHWARDEN AND VESTRY ACCOUNTS, 1690 (DRO EP/MER 34)
(COURTESY OF DURHAM COUNTY RECORD OFFICE AND THE INCUMBENT PARISH OF MERRINGTON)

'May ye 13th: 1696. The Churchwardens of ye
Parish of Church Merrington did agree with Henry
Richardson of ye old bailey in Durham, Plummer, to repaint
the seeds of ye parish Church of Church Merrington, for which he is to have
Twenty five shillings. And for after six years next following, he is to uphold and
keep ye said seeds
(so far as belongs to ye said parish) ...
for which he ye Henry Richardson is to have
sixteen shillings every year. In witness
with ye Churchwardens and ye Henry Richardson
have [subscribed] their names ye day and year
... about.

Martin White
John Brass   Churchwardens'

In 1713, he is chosen as churchwarden during Easter.

PARISH OF MERRINGTON – CHURCHWARDEN AND VESTRY ACCOUNTS, 1713 (DRO EP/MER 34)
(COURTESY OF DURHAM COUNTY RECORD OFFICE AND THE INCUMBENT PARISH OF MERRINGTON)

'Church-wardens chosen on Easter Tuesday 1713.
Merrington – Martin White
Ferry-hill – John Brass
Chilton – Thomas Dunn of West Close
Hett – George Jackson'

Perhaps John Brass felt guilty for bringing Andrew Mills into and destroying his family, hence the reason he sought out the church as his comfort. Perhaps he wanted to be closer to his children, for he was heartbroken and wanted to visit his children's tomb regularly.

In 1703, John Brass appears to be petitioning in respect of a local quarry. (*DCD/K/LP7/9 – 15, Durham University Archives and Special Collections*)

Re-marriage in 1704

In December 1703, John's wife Margaret dies. In less than 6 months, on May 16th, 1704, he is remarried to an Elizabeth Humble of Ferryhill, in the church of St Mary-Le-Bow, Durham City. The marriage is recorded in both parish registers.

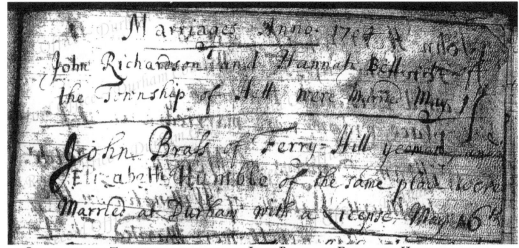

'[1704] John Brass of Ferry-Hill yeoman, and
Elizabeth Humble of the same place were
Married at Durham with a licence May 16'

It may be possible to say, although it is not conclusive, that a re-marriage to someone so shortly after the first wife's death meant that John may have found someone else to love whilst he was still originally married, mostly likely whilst he was working as a churchwarden. This only option was to wait until his first wife Margaret passed away so he would not seen to commit the act of bigamy.

THE TOMBSTONE OF JOHN AND MARGARET BRASS, AND THE GRAVESTONE OF ELIZABETH BUSTON
(AUTHOR'S PHOTOGRAPH)

Death of John Brass

John and Elizabeth Brass remained in Ferryhill. On the 22nd January 1722 (O.S) 1723 (N.S), John Brass passes away, leaving a house and a garth in Tudhoe to his brother in law and wife, and a small sum of money to his widow, Elizabeth Brass (*Durham University Probate Records, DPR/I/1/1722/B12/1-2*). Interestingly, John is buried with his first wife Margaret.

'Here lies the body of John Brass, of Ferryhill
Who departed this life Jan 22nd day, 1722'

Elizabeth, his second wife, appears with an alternative surname Buston on the gravestone. She is buried next to John and Margaret, in a separate grave. She dies Nov 19th, 1758.

'Here lieth the body of Elizabeth Buston,
Who departed this life Nov 19th, 1758, aged 86'

If this Elizabeth Buston were the same Elizabeth Humble of 1704, she would have been aged 32 years of age when she married John Brass. However John Brass may have been well into his late sixties or early seventies. She would have been half his age. No wonder why he married outside the parish of Merrington.

So ends the tragic story of a family torn apart by murder, whose surviving parents were torn apart by grief, of a man drawn to the church, and redemption in younger love by marriage.

Part Four

'Awake the god of day'

Chapter 13
'The ...erring sprit hies To his confine'

The Brass Murders of 1682 left a mental impact on the residents of Ferryhill and the surrounding occupants for many centuries to come.

The 18th Century

The Brass Grave and William (Wily) Lynn of Merrington

In 1789, more than a hundred years since the children were laid to rest in the churchyard of Kirk Merrington, their grave was restored by a gentleman named George Wood, who was a Senior Proctor of the Consistory of Durham. Robert Surtees remarked on the restoration:

> 'He restored Brass' tomb, but he chose to state that it was done by parochial subscription, and he gave the old parish register a gallant new cover of Russia, wisely considering that a good coat sometimes saved a honest man from neglect'

The most insightful thing about the children's tombstone after the restoration was that the words *'executed and'* were scratched out, leaving only the words *'hung in chains'* alone. Some people believe that the murderer's father did this, that he walked to Kirk Merrington, and with his walking stick, attempted to remove this part of this inscription, as part of trying to redeem his son's fate. However, history is wiser than people, and according to James Dodd, author of *'The History of the Urban District of Spennymoor'* (1897), an innkeeper called Wily Lynn, who owned the Bay Horse Inn, at Kirk Merrington, (now a private house on Merrington Lane) was often fond of argument, particularly that of the fate of Andrew Mills, that he was not executed first, and then hung in chains, but was simply hung in chains alive. He then went nightly to the churchyard, which stood a hundred feet away, and began to remove the words to validate his belief.

James Dodds tells more of this man's eccentricities, but a remarkable fact that on his last will and testament, dated 6 June 1835 (*Durham University Family Records DPR/I/1/1839/L14/1-2*), a William Lynn, farmer of Merrington, leaves a staggering amount of money to his remaining family. His estate was worth £1,500 in 1839 on his death; today his estate would be worth in excess of £800,000.

The 19th Century

Andrew Mills' Stob (1683 – 1840)

For over 150 years, the gibbet that once hung Andrew Mills in an iron cage stood approximately a mile north of Ferryhill, in full site of the farmhouse on the western hill. As the gibbet cage had disappeared into the annals of time, the wooden post remained on the landscape.

Too, as the years rolled by, the facts of why the murder happened and how the murderer was punished began to dissolve away into folklore and legend.

Charles Waterton, a noted 18ᵗʰ century naturalist and explorer, spent his youth at a school in Tudhoe, Spennymoor, and it is here that he recalls his childhood of growing up with the tale of the murders, in the book 'Essays of Natural History', 1838.

> 'Betwixt Tudhoe School and Ferry Hill, there stood an oaken post, very strong, and some nine feet high. This was its appearance in my days, but formerly it must have been much higher. It was known to all the country round by the name of Andrew Mills' stob. We often went to see it, and one afternoon, whilst we were looking at it, an old woman came up, took her knife from her pocket, and then pared off a chip, which she then carefully folded up in a bit of paper. She said it was good for curing the toothache.
>
> A neighbouring farmer and his wife had gone a tea-drinking one summer afternoon, leaving six children behind. Andrew Mills, the servant-man, fancied he would become heir of the farmer's property if the children were only got out of the way. So he cut all their throats, and his body was hung in chains on this noted stob. The poor children were all buried in one grave in a neighbouring churchyard. The tombstone tells their melancholy fate...'

The oaken post remained until the 1840s, when a 'Mr Laverick' removed the post entirely, and enclosed the land, returning the section of the Great North Road to its former beauty, instead of a place of mystery and curiosity. This is further evidence that in the 1851 census of Ferryhill, there is a gentleman called Thomas Laverick, who was recorded as a land agent.

The Theatrical Play

In James Dodds' book 'The History of the Urban District of Spennymoor' (1897), the author recalls that:

> 'Some years ago, a local playwright dramatized the story for the Spennymoor theatre, and it drew immense houses. It has frequently been performed in booths and theatres, and whenever it is revived in the district, so strong is the local interest in this tragedy of two hundred years ago, that the theatre was crowded in every performance'.

For the first time ever since the play was written over a hundred years ago, a full copy of the script is laid bare for the reader, courtesy of the British Library Board.

Whilst most of the original play is decipherable, there are certain words or sentences of the play that were hard to make out, so required modernisation, for the benefit of the reader. These sections have been put in *italics*. Characters have been put in order of appearance. Also, Act One has been split into two for more dramatic effect, and Act Two has become Act Three.

Chapter 14

The 1876 Theatre Play

'Andrew Mills, Legend of Spennymoor'

Written by W. Stephens: *A dramatic play*, founded on events that occurred in 1632 [1682] – characters *in order of appearance*:

Paul Lovel, an old gypsy
John Brass, farmer, father, and master
Margaret Brass, wife of John Brass, and mother
Andrew Mills, a manservant to John Brass
Sarah Lightfoot, a maid to Margaret Brass
Becky Buttercup, a maid to Margaret Brass
Simon, a stable boy to John Brass.
An Officer of the Law.
The Governor of the Prison.
Include Villagers, and Wardens of the Prison.

Act One

I: Upon The Four Lane Ends, *a road*

Music, Hurry. Paul enters, angry.

Paul: Ah, I have outsmarted them, the cowards. Dogs. Do did they think that age had stiffened my limbs and rendered me incapable even at flight – ah, dogs. House dwelling dogs. They shall suffer this gypsy's curse, it shall cling to them until it is extinguished in death. And for him, their leader who once walked upon the earth and was been a king among his people, a leader of his race, for him and on him my curse is three times doubled. Ah, for the days of my lost youth. Oh, for the strength that has fled from me. That long ago I had the vigour. That once well within this frame the boldest of my foes should have bit the dust. But I am old; my strength has fled. This old gypsy can but suffer, but I shall not be silent. No, I still have the strength to curse, to curse, to curse...

John enters.

John: What be the matter old man and who are you cursing?

Paul: Those who have usurped me.

John: You are old, on the verge of the grave. Old age should be more forgiven. Are we not taught to forgive those among us as we hope to be forgiven?

Paul: That is the Christian's belief – I am not your people. I am not of your faith.

John: This is the faith of all good men – no matter what their belief.

Paul: Then I am not good – yet I can say that I have never harmed a living soul yet those who have injured me –

John: Come, who has usurped you?

Paul: I shall answer you. I see here a deep wrong, and it is from one who you have warmed your heart and is sheltering with you. He will sting you like the serpent. Beware of such a one.

John: I know of no one, so. But come with me. You're weak and feeble. My dwelling is not far off. Lean on my arm, I will lead you to it. Here, drink from this, (hands over a small flask), it will revive you. Now come.

Paul: Stop – his name is...

John: Come, My *farmhouse* is *on the hill*. My help is near...

Paul: No, not there. Beneath that roof dwells one who has ever done to me a bitter wrong. I would not cross the threshold of the house that shelters him.

John: Do you mean my farm servant Andrew Mills?

Paul: Yes, beware of that man – Oh my, your future – It is useless to warn you. Fate decrees that it must be fulfilled, yet time will come and you will remember my words. Aye, remember them with vain regret, think of them in bitter sorrow.

John: These are but wild ramblings. Age and health have *dampened your reason. Please,* accept the kindness I *offer* you.

Paul: You have been kind, and for that I thank you. May one day I *will* repay the debt. Only *that* my warning will *not prevent* you from a cruel blow which will strike those *who* you hold most dear – I can at least help you to *revenge.* Farewell, we shall meet again *soon* and then...

John: But...

Paul: You will need my aid and you shall have it. Farewell, till then. Farewell.

Paul exits, music.

John: Strange his warning, *and* against Andrew too. The best, the most faithful servant I have ever had – Ah, I suppose Andrew is his *ways* must have driven him off the farm and so offended the old man – well, well, I would take a deal to make me think *boldly* of Andrew – *by the way,* I think Andrew has a fondness of our maid, Sarah Lightfoot. I will *ask* him upon the subject and if I find my suspicions are correct, I will try to make *them* happy, he shall have the little cottage at Four Lane Ends and my wife Margaret will give a helping *hand* towards furnishing it *out* for *them. She* is a good kind-hearted soul and *has not* objected to my spending some of my wife's old uncle's legacy in making the *deal.* Five hundred pounds, it's a good sum and all in gold too. *I shall go to Durham to obtain it.* Providence has smiled on me. A well *family, three* dear little children that I love, a well-stocked farm, and now Five hundred pounds. *I have had no* bad crops, *but* a fine harvest, *and* yet the gypsy has *surprised* me – but *I shall not think of him, but only of my wife, my children, and the help that wants me. I must go and be quick.*

John exits, music.

II. At Kitchen *window*, Interior of Farm

Margaret: *The day is drawing in* rapidly *and the sun is sinking in the west, and* yet he has not arrived home – *should any harm befall him – my heart sinks within me.* What is someone knew of my husband's errand, and of the large amount of money. What if *some evil disposed some person to rob and murder? This suspense is terrible. I will go to the door and look – no sign of him – oh, heaven guard my dear husband and send him home* safely – *is it he, no, it is only Andrew.*

Music, **Andrew** enters.

Margaret: Any sign of your master, yet?
Andrew: No, mistress (why is she so anxious?) He will come back, mistress. Why should you be so fearful? Master has gone to Durham and come back safe many a time than this.
Margaret: But never on such an errand.
Andrew: What errand, mistress?
Margaret: (oh, what have I said, John charged me to keep the object of his journey secret from all). It is nothing that concerns you, Andrew. It is his farm business, nothing else.
Andrew: (There is a secret and I will find it out.)
Margaret: What was the noise I heard just now?
Andrew: An old gypsy thief who was prowling to steal what he could first lay his hands on. I chased him from the farm and he cursed me   He was fit for his age. Did you hear him, mistress?
Margaret: I heard voices in anger. Andrew, you should have given him food, not threats.
Andrew: Please, mistress, do not blame me for being faithful to my master. He was prowling for anything but food. These gypsies are bad. Think of them. As an honest servant, I can but only do my duty to my master.
Margaret: I believe you to be honest and faithful. Next time you see a poor beggar, it is your master's interest that you offer them kind charity. There will not be bad substance in our dwelling. If we share our belongings with those who want – they suffer enough, gypsy or no gypsy, old or poor. Next time he comes, help him. Remember this.
Andrew: I will obey you, mistress. I am sorry that I have angered you.
Margaret: Not angered me, you acted as you thought best for your master. That will excuse all.
Andrew: I am glad I have not offended you, good mistress. I was about to ask something of you.
Margaret: *Of me?*
Andrew: Yes, mistress. Miss Sarah Lightfoot. I have loved her for a long time and yet she seems to shun me of late. Would you put in a good word for me? A word from you would go a long way, mistress.
Margaret: Can you not speak to her yourself? You do not need me to ask her for you, do you?
Andrew: No, mistress, but you have influence. One word would do so much.
Margaret: Well them, I shall speak that word, for I believe you will make a good and worthy husband.
Andrew: Thank you, *mistress.*

Margaret: Not now for thanks. I have my husband's help. His well-known voice will give another good, Andrew. Ah, my husband arrives. Let me be the first to greet him.

Margaret exits.

Andrew: Good Andrew, she says. Ah, if she knew of the rage in my heart, she'd not do me good. Within me burns every hatred and rage. Fiercer if repressed. Yet a fire consumes me – what a life! Condemned to wear these; to hide my features with smiles; to be happy for the food I eat and that I live here in this very farmhouse, where once my father was the master, and which he was cast out by my master's father. Master, I hate the word. I was born to rule, not serve. To govern... I hate him for being my master; hate him for the happiness he enjoys; his wife; children; his business. I will continue to smile, as fortune will change. Meanwhile, I shall play the faithful servant, who is quiet and content, who is like a well-taught dog; licks the hand that feeds him; but a good dog that one-day will bite.

Music, Sarah enters.

Sarah: A dog bite. Bite whom, Andrew?
Andrew: (Oh, she overheard me.) I was speaking of a mad dog *that* I have heard *has been* prowling *about*, and...
Sarah: A mad dog. I shall be afraid to stir out of doors with the children. A mad dog – I hope it won't bite me.
Andrew: No fear of that, lass. I will protect you.
Sarah: You're very good, Andrew, but I'd rather not stand in need of *your* protection.
Andrew: I would willingly protect you, my lass, with my life. Why do you turn from me? If you knew the story this heart would tell. Sarah, I urge you to be mine. Can you not trust me?
Sarah: Trust you with what?
Andrew: Your heart. Ah, Sarah, listen to me. It is in your power to make. It is my destiny to make me a good man, as our master is to make of me.
Sarah: This from you, whom all people call 'good'?
Andrew: *Yes*, from me. We are not masters of our own lives. *Others often form our future for us.* I have had temptations and often heard voices *whispering* in my ear; things *that make me shudder.* You have even calmed the fierce anguish of my soul. *With you*, I could be content to live a life of humble labour. Be to me my *loving* angel. Do not *reject* my love.
Sarah: Andrew, you terrify me.
Andrew: I would not terrify you. I would *love and cherish you*. It is my honesty that tells you. *My love is so fierce* that it might turn to bitterness and hate.
Sarah: Hate, Andrew?
Andrew: Yes, hate. Love is akin to hate. If I had thought you loved another, I could find it in my heart to kill him and you.
Sarah: Please, Andrew, *restrain yourself.*
Andrew: (I have said too much). Forgive my sad passion. Say that you'll be mine and that *it* will be well between us?

Sarah: You're so young. I *do not know* what to say. Tomorrow Andrew – dear Andrew – I'll give *you* my answer.

(**Margaret**, without, shouts: Sarah, Sarah)

Sarah: *My mistress calls for me.* Tomorrow Andrew, tomorrow...

Sarah exits.

Andrew: (Dear Andrew she said. Did she really think me a fool that I spoke so freely? The mask falls, though only for a moment. Oh, that I were rich that I could have her love. I will in some way, but how, how?)

John and **Margaret** enter.

Andrew: Ah, master. Welcome home.

John: Thanks Andrew. I am glad for myself to be once more safe beneath my own roof (takes out wallet).

Andrew: You have had a heavy load to carry, master (drops bag, *inside some gold sound*)

Margaret: Do not meddle with that bag, Andrew, as it does not concern you.

John: I could trust this lad fifty times, with the sum being in honest Andrew's hands. The danger was on the road, dear wife, not here were all are honest around us – there is no more need for further *concern* and Andrew, I am sure you will rejoice at my good fortune. This bag contains a legacy *of* five hundred pounds, all in guineas. My wife's uncle bequeathed *it to me* and which Lawyer Todd of Durham *asked me to collect only from today.*

Andrew: (Five hundred pounds. *Only* would it be mine.)

John: Madge here has been telling me of your *worry*, Andrew. Fear not, man, you shall be happy if we can make it so.

Andrew: Five hundred pounds.

John: You seem dazed.

Andrew: Your pardon, master. I meant to say I give you five hundred grateful thanks. (Five hundred pounds, *only* would it be mine)

John: *Here,* wife, take the bag and lock it in the old chest under the bed. We can say we sleep on gold *from now on.*

Margaret: Do not jest, *John.* I seem to feel a foreboding that this gold will not bring about happiness.

John: Well then, I shall begin to wish *we had not* received it. Come wife, go lock it up safely.

Margaret: I will, and put our dear children to bed at the same time.

Margaret exits.

John: Andrew, see to the stables, and then to supper and to bed, for I am tired from my day's journey. Why Margaret, you've left the bag on the table. She is like all *mothers,* thinks more of her children, than all of the money in the world.

John takes up bag, exits.

Andrew: (Five hundred pounds. Now if it were mine, what could I do with it, so it would grow within my hands? I would make it a foundation of a fortune. Why should they have all and I have nothing – that voice whispers in my ear, 'take, take it. Kill all, take it' – I shudder at myself. 'Get thee behind me, Satan'. Oh, let me *out* into the open, as I seem to choke within these walls, and try to shake off this strong feeling.)

Music, **Andrew** rushes out, exits.

Sarah enters.

Sarah: There, whilst mistress is singing the dear children to sleep, let me think so. Love Andrew let me ask my heart. I can hardly answer – he is so *up front* and course in his ways – he terrified me just now. And then, what did that handsome gentleman who I met in the village say that he loved me, that he would make a lady of me, to marry me. It must be very nice to be a lady and to have someone in want of me, and yet if I reject Andrew, I will break his heart. Oh, it is gratifying to one's vanity to have two sweethearts, but rather perplexing for I can't marry him. (A clock strikes eight.) 8 o'clock, the time I promised to meet the other. Well, I'll just step out, and there will be no harm in wondering what he has to say and that will help me make up my mind.

Music, **Sarah** exits.

III. At Kitchen *table*, Interior of Farm

Becky and **Simon** enter.

Becky: Tell me, Simon. I don't like to be followed about by boys.
Simon: Boys indeed? My father says that all boys are like their fathers, and that's what I mean to be.
Becky: You, a father, indeed?
Simon: And why not, my father had thirteen children. A baker's dozen.
Becky: Your mother, you mean.
Simon: Well, man and wife are one flesh, so it is the same.
Becky: Thirteen children?
Simon: Yes, and eight pair of them are twins.
Becky: Poor woman, she must have gone through a great deal.
Simon: I believe you. She was an awful woman as I've found out many times. She was heavy fisted, was mother.
Becky: Such a prospect.
Simon: Yes, but an inviting one, beauty is, and I mean to follow my father's example.
Becky: But you're so little.
Simon: I am not done growing yet.
Becky: But you're so young.

Simon: I shall mend to that every day.

Becky: But you couldn't keep a wife?

Simon: Yah, but I could. I've got arms and I could work, plough, saw, feed animals and tend horses...I've been practising...I've got my hands in proper.

Becky: I am afraid you know too much.

Simon: Marry me and I will make you as mine.

Becky: Ah, Simon. I think that influence is on many subjects and matrimony is of them.

Simon: Ah, don't say that Becky.

Becky: Well, you live in hope.

Simon: Then I shan't die in despair, just *please kiss me* to bind the bargain.

Becky: Sir, a kiss indeed? No, that would be *foolish*. Well you may have one. (She *gently* kisses his lips)

Simon: Though it's naughty, yet it's nice. I will look to have a kiss like that every five minutes.

Becky: Hush, here's master and mistress.

Music, **John** and **Margaret** enters.

John: Safely stowed away. Now Becky, make supper, and you boy, go call Andrew in and then let's have supper, and to bed.

Simon: Yes, master. I will always be ready *with* my whistles.

Simon exits.

Becky makes supper.
Sarah enters.

Margaret: You have been out again, Sarah, I see. It is late and –

John: Say, don't scold – Andrew and her, you understand wife. We courted ourselves once.

Sarah: Andrew indeed.

John: A lover's quarrel, I suspect.

Margaret: Don't tease the girl. Come get your suppers.

They sit and eat.

John: Where can Andrew be?

Simon re-enters.

Simon: I have just seen him master. He was talking to a man outside. My supper, Becky.

Simon sits in corner seat. **Becky** gives him supper.

John: Who could the man be, so late? Ah, here he comes.

Andrew enters.

John: What kept you so late, Andrew? Who was the man with you, just now?

Andrew: (Now for my *ploy*.) He brought a letter, sir, and for you.

John: Did he not wait for an answer?

Andrew: No, he said the letter would explain and he was in haste – something about life and death – and galloped off.

John: Life and death – really? (*opens and scans letter*) Ill news, indeed. It is from your mother. Your poor father *is* ill dying. What shall we do?

Margaret: My father. I'll....Oh, let me fly to his side.

John: But our children, Madge. Can we leave them alone?

Margaret: Our servants will watch over them. John, you stay here, let me go alone.

John: What, through this dark night - that *you shall* not. I have it. Andrew can stay and guard the house until I come back. The distance is not far. Simon, go and put the old mare in the cart. Hasten.

Simon: Bother that mare; I'll sooner have my supper.

Simon exits.

John: I'll see you to your mother's and then hasten back. Andrew, I leave you to guard this house during my short away. I know I can trust you with *my newfound wealth* and that my precious treasure, my children.

Andrew: Fear not for me, sir. I'll guard your house as faithfully as it belonged to me.

John: I am sure of it. I have an award for you. You have been a good and faithful servant, and

—

Andrew: I want no reward, sir, for always doing my duty for such a good master.

Simon re-enters.

Simon: Old mare is in the cart, master. Now I'll have my supper.

John: Come, wife.

Margaret: Let me kiss my children. *I will go now.*

Margaret exits.

Sarah: Do not go, master.

John: Why not – oh, I suppose you're afraid of being left alone in this old house alone, but Andrew will keep you company. *You can* sit up until I return.

Sarah: Oh, sir, forgive me for *speaking plainly* sir, but I implore you not to go till morning.

John: But this is urgent. I shall be back in a few hours, two probably. You will have Andrew, Simon, and Becky in the house with you. There is no cause for fear.

Sarah: I do not say I fear, sir, but yet some feeling I know not what but a dread foreboding urges me to implore you not to go until morning.

John: Nonsense, girl. Duty calls your mistress's to be at her dying father's bed. My duty as her husband bids me to accompany her.

Margaret re-enters.

Margaret: I have kissed our children. Ah John, dear husband, as I bent over them a voice seemed to whisper to me that I might not again see them in life.

John: What *has* come over you, women. Here's Sarah imploring me not to go and now your fretting over the children. We can't take them with us. What harm can be done to them in our absence?

Margaret: You are right. It was a weakness and I must overcome it. Come, my poor father, may the Lord grant that I find him living.

John: Look after the place, Andrew, until I return. Come wife.

Music, John and Margaret exits.

Andrew: (So far, so well. In two hours, I may have much, so very much. That treasure, I must have it, but how to get rid of that boy?)

Simon: Won't you have your supper, Andrew?

Andrew: I cannot eat.

Simon: Then I will eat it for you. (Eats.)

Betty: You're in love or you've got the toothache that you cannot eat with. If it's love, Sarah can cure you of that, if its toothache, I have some laudanum in the closet. It's a capital cure.

Andrew: (In a devilish thought.) You're right, Becky. You have guessed the cause of my suffering. *My gums are raging*. It affects me terribly.

Becky: I'll soon cure that.

Becky exits.

Becky re-enters with a bottle in her hand, and hands it to Andrew.

Becky: There, put that on your gums, it will soothe the pain. Don't swallow it though, or you will sleep for a week.

Andrew: (Can I get her to drink, and the boy too? I'll try).

Becky: Now glutton, when you are done eating, it is time you went to bed.

Simon: But I am not half done!

Andrew secretly pours some of the laudanum into cups, and tops it over with beer.

Andrew: Before you go, you will drink a glass of ale, won't you to our dear master and mistress, and may her dear father is well soon?

Becky: Oh, I will drink to that (drinks).

Simon: So will I (drinks).

Andrew: Come, Sarah, will you not drink?

Sarah: To such a pledge, yes. (Drinks slightly).

Andrew: (She has scarcely drank?) Drink it up.

Sarah: The beer has a strange taste. I do not like it.

Simon: Don't you? I do. I will drink yours for you.

Becky: Oh, you pig. Come, sir, to bed.

Simon: Yes, my dear, let's go to bed.

Becky: Why you're half tipsy. A nice husband you'll make – no, not my way, sir. That side of the house is your road.

Simon: Come and tuck me up, Becky.

Becky: Go to bed you fool, do.

Becky pushes Simon off. Simon exits.

Becky: Ah, I declare I feel awful drowsy myself. I'll just like down and have forty winks. Well I do feel sleepy. Are you coming Sarah?

Sarah: I promised master that I would wait up till his return.

Becky: Well you can wait up. I will be so afraid to sleep by myself upstairs.

Sarah: I will join you presently.

Becky: All right. Good night, Mr Andrew. I hope in the morning your toothache will be gone.

Andrew: Good night.

Becky: Good night. Well I am sleepy.

Becky ascends stairs, exits.

Andrew: At *last* alone, Sarah.

Sarah: Do not talk *with me now* for I feel drowsy. Let me have a few moments *shut-eye* in this chair.

Andrew: (The ale was well drugged. She scarcely drank it and yet sleep has already overcome her. Let me wait awhile and when I know she sleeps, it will satisfy my fears).

Music. Sarah sleeps. Andrew cautiously approaches her.

Andrew: (What was that she hid in her heart this evening? I fear she is *playing* false. I will be satisfied.)

Andrew draws Sarah's locket from her bosom.

Andrew: (It is a portrait, and that of a rival. *I am almost certain*, I recognise the features of the man she met in the wood tonight. False girl. Well I'll give one more chance, but the gold, let me gain that and then to ask her to become my companion in my flight. If she refuses, woe is to her. Now for the gold. Master will stare when he finds his treasure gone and his honest servant gone also – the *gullible* fool, he should guard his money better.)

Andrew takes candle from the table.

Andrew: (She sleeps again. I hear those voices, they say 'here's a chance. This is the golden moment, seize upon it. The gold will give you a new start in life in some other land'. Shall I lose it? No. He can well spare it. If I lose this precious moment, I will be to my loss again. 'Under the bed', did he say? Ah, now for my last chance. If this fails, I am lost. She still sleeps. How silent is this place? I can almost hear my heart beat. It is as silent as the grave – the grave, let me not think of that. No, think of life and life's enjoyments and what gold can buy. Gold, that *word* has renewed me.)

Andrew moves towards the hallway. Curtains close.

Intermission.

Act Two
Originally part of Act One, broken for dramatic effect.

I. At Kitchen *table*, Interior of Farm

Curtains open.
Pause. Sarah awakens.

Sarah: Have I been sleeping? Where am I here? It was a dream, but oh, how terrible. I think that the dear children and myself were on a boat upon the waters, so smooth and fair, when Andrew appeared and hurled them one by one into the water which turned into a river of blood. Oh, dreadful. Terrible. Then he seized hold of me, and with his touch, I woke up. Thank Heaven, it was just a dream, but oh, how terrible...

A noise is heard within.

Andrew: (speaks without) Hush little imps or I'll...

Sarah: What noise is that? Andrew? And in my master's bed chamber? What can he want in there? My dream! Oh, horrible! Let me know of this dread. This dreaded truth. Even though it may cost me my life.

Music, Sarah crosses to the door, sinks to her knees and prays.

Sarah: Oh, Heaven give me strength. Yet I scarcely dare to look, a cold chill is in my heart. Ah, my dream is realised! There is Andrew, like a demon contemplating his work! Oh, accursed gold! My masters! He has the bag of money in his hand! Oh, he again uplifts the fatal knife and ... Forbear! Murderer! Oh, Heaven, give me strength to struggle and save their lives.

Sarah enters the room.

II. In The Master Bedroom, Interior of Farm

Sarah re-appears with Andrew.

Andrew: You know all (*throws her off.*)
Sarah: All, murderer, all!
Andrew: Murderer! That has sealed your doom.
Sarah: Must I die too?
Andrew: You must or I...yet one chance of life I'll give ... you see this gold, I have gained it at what a terrible price.
Sarah: The lives of three innocents who have never harmed you.
Andrew: You were the cause!
Sarah: Me?
Andrew: Yes, for you! I needed gold and meant to fly with it to some distant land and to make you my companion in my flight! My love you made me become a robber, worse, a murderer! I thought to lure you with this money which a life of toil we would never have to do again. Hear me, one of the children woke, it was old enough to speak *and* to tell the tale that it has seen me with the bag of money in my grasp. I could not resist the dreaded impulse that engaged my knife against its heart. It fell back dead. Then a voice whispered, 'Kill all, make sure of it!' – I became mad! – I did kill them!
Sarah: Monster!
Andrew: But it was for you! Listen, here is gold, fly with me. There are horses in the stables. We can fly before the deed is known. From Sunderland, many a ship sails. Come with me, this gold shall be yours in some foreign land. My sin will not be known and we will forget my curse, knowing it was for you.
Sarah: Never, monster, never! Become a thing as guilty as yourself? No, it is mine to avenge this task. I'll denounce you for this deed, murderer as you are. There are those above who will hear my voice. What Ho! Murder! Help!
Andrew: Silence! Their drink was drugged. They live, you not.
Sarah: Oh, villain! Villain! (*She rushes towards Andrew.*)
Andrew: Your life is not that way, unless it is with me.
Sarah: With you, monster? Child murderer? *I'll face* death sooner.
Andrew: Then death is it.

Music, Andrew seizes Sarah. They struggle.

Sarah: Oh, help...Mercy, Andrew, forbear. You said you loved me?
Andrew: But you love me not, you love another! He *and* you met tonight. His portrait is within your breast. You would denounce me, you have said it. You must die. I cannot spare you.
Sarah: Then I will not die without at least one struggle for my life.

Music, Sarah breaks away from Andrew. He peruses her. Pulls her down, stabs her.

Andrew: It is done... It is done... Ah, my hands are red.

The window in flat is open and **Paul Lovel** is seen through it.

Andrew: Let me go and cleanse my hands. Ah, it is you.
Paul: Murderer!
Andrew: That word has sealed your doom. Die you.

Andrew picks up his master's pistol and fires. **Paul** is seen to fall.

Andrew: My voices, ah, what whisper they? 'Hide the money and fix the guilt on him'. (*He opens trap in floor and places the bag inside and shuts it.*) Here, there. The farmer would never think of looking for his treasure beneath his very feet. Now for the old gypsy. He is but senseless, not dead. I'll swear he did it. Better that than flight.

Andrew opens door, brings **Paul** in senseless, and lies him down.

Andrew: I hear voices without. It is my master. Now to give the alarm. Say, let me wound myself slightly; it will give a colour to my tale. (*Forces himself with knife.*) What Ho! Murder! Help! Murder!

Hurried music, **Andrew** sinks in chair.

III. Within *The Hallway*, Interior of Farm

John and **Margaret** enter, with villagers.
Simon and **Becky** enter from above.

John: What alarm is this? (*Rushes into chamber room.*) Ah, what scene of blood and horror meets my sight! Ah, Sarah is dead! (*Returns to passage way.*) You wounded this old gypsy who is too senseless to speak. Andrew, what means it? Who has done this?
Andrew: I know not, see I am slain master. Yet I killed one of them... ah, he is here!
Margaret: Tell me my children?
Andrew: I was sleeping by the fire, tired with work. I heard a noise and woke. I saw you a hoary ruffian bending over Sarah, a blood stained knife in his hand. And I see two others escaping by the window. I seized him, he stabbed me, but I had the strength to fire your old pistol at him. Faintness came over me and I fell back. I know no more.
Margaret: Ah, husband, the gold! Robbers have been here! My children! Let me assure myself of their safety (*Rushes into chamber room, a loud scream is heard, she re-enters.*) Oh John, husband. Our children! All dead! All dead! The chest has been broken and the accused gold has gone. Oh, what a sight to great a mother's eyes!
John: My children! All accursed monsters! And this poor girl who doubtlessly fell defending them. Weep on wife, it is for women to weep, and for men to avenge. At least one of them is in my power. He stirs.... he moves... Look old miscreant at your work!

Paul (*reviving*.): Not mine! No, not mine! I came to warn, to save... I am innocent! Gods of my race, hear me, swear this blood is not of my shedding! No, not mine!

John: To a prison with him, and now to hunt the others to their deaths.

Andrew: (I am safe.)

Margaret: My children, my poor children! What shall comfort me now?

Andrew: Heaven will console you, dear mistress. You will meet your murdered innocents there.

Paul: You *fibber*, but this old gipsy will fool you yet.

Picture in, the curtains close.

Intermission.

Act Three

Originally entitled Act Two.

I. In the yard, exterior of Farmhouse

Originally noted as a street, works better if outside of farmhouse.

Curtains open.
Church bells toll at intervals. **Andrew** enters.

Andrew: (Curse those bells, how dismal they toll. Ding Dong Ding Dong. It is for their funeral. They wanted me to go to it but I told them that my grief for her was too great It was a lie, I feared to look at her coffin. I have hidden the money but have not dared to move it, but tonight I will. All will be quiet. The window shutter be easily moved when all are hushed in sleep. I can enter, get my spoil, and then make some excuse in a day or so to leave this place, but not hurriedly, that would excite suspicion. (*Bells*) Again those sound. Let me have some brandy to nerve me, to give me courage. I never drank before in all my life but I do need it now for that girl is ever before my eyes. Her death scream ever ringing in my ears. Murderer! Murderer! Let me drink and forget it. Ah, can I ever forget...)

Simon enters, wearing large hat.

Simon: Eh, master Andrew are you there?

Andrew: Whence come you, why do you wear that?

Simon: Oh, this is a bit of mourning. Becky put it on me out of respect for Sarah and...

Andrew: Name her not...Name her not...

Simon: Ah, it is a tender subject with you. Ah, Mr Andrew, you should have been there at the burying. All of the village were there and then when the parson gave out the text for the funeral, there wasn't a dry eye among the lot.

Andrew: What was the text?

Simon: Thou shalt do no murder.

Andrew: Oh, horrible. Silence. Cease your idle chatter. That text will be forever engraved here on my brain. I cannot bear the thought. Give me brandy, or I shall choke.

Andrew rushed into house, exits.

Simon: Idle chatter – well his grief has turned his brain surely - a grief's a dreadful thing. I must have a pill to wash mine down. Sorrow's day. I'll go and give mine a wet.

Simon exits.

Paul enters.

Paul: He is here, I saw him now for my just step. Let me try the effect of a word on him. It will sling his conscience keener than a dagger's sheaf.

Andrew re-enters outside.

Andrew: I have drunk glass after glass. I'll drink no more lest I betray myself.
Paul: All the drink of the world will not draw your conscience, Andrew Mills.
Andrew: Ah, old raven, you are there.
Paul: A raven, am I? Well, I'll croak on your gibbet yet.
Andrew: Your own you meant. You are not out of danger yet.
Paul: Danger? Look well to yourself. The gallows yearns for you. All the gold that you have hidden will not save you from that... from that...
Andrew: Gold says you. This will stop your tongue forever.

Andrew seizes Paul, by rushing on him with uplifted knife. Simon re-enters, and stops Andrew.

Simon: What against an old man, Andrew, and knife too? For shame, Andrew. For shame.
Paul: He has no shame. See there on the blade of the knife, there's blood, her blood.
Simon: Whose?
Paul: The blood of the victims. Tell him how it came there?
Andrew: Oh, horrible! Horrible!

Picture, close in

II. On The Four Lane Ends, *a road*

Andrew enters.

Andrew: I must fly from this place and tonight. I fear detection – my coolness has deserted me. I fear I will betray myself, that gypsy would. I could silence him. My scheme of throwing the burden of guilt on him has failed, but I will not fly without my gold. In yonder barn I will try to asleep awhile till night and then for the money I've hidden, and afterwards flight. My voices urge me, 'Hark!', they speak plainly, 'Flee this spot or vengeance will overtake you'. But it is too late to retrace my steps. I must go on, it is my destiny.

Andrew exits.

III. At Kitchen *table,* Interior of Farm

John sits at table, reading a book out loud.
Margaret walks about the kitchen.
Simon and **Becky** are preparing to leave.

John: See dear wife, here are some words of comfort. Go now to rest, I will be with you.
Simon: Good night, master. Oh, Becky, I shall be dreaming of prophecies all night.
Becky: Get you to bed, you *silly bugger,* and dream of your dinner tomorrow. That will suit you best.

Simon and Becky exit.

John: Come wife, go you to bed. I will soon be with you.
Margaret: I shall not sleep.
John: Only now I wish it.
Margaret: Your will is law – I will go to sleep. No, I will think of my children and weep.

Margaret exits. **John** watches her off.

A tap is heard at door, **John** opens it. **Paul** and an **Officer** enters.

John: I have consented to watch unknowingly to my wife, but I fear that this scheme will fail. First, I do not believe him guilty; next, I have examined every crevice narrowly and can discern no trace of a hiding place.
Paul: His father dwelt here before yours did. He knows this building better than you. As of him coming here, he must, it is his destiny. I have used a spell of potency, it will draw him here with a resistless pawing. Guilt like his is his own doom. Hush, I hear footsteps without. It is he. Conceal yourself quickly.

Music, they hide. **Andrew** enters through window, he is sleeping.

Andrew: John, I have followed my voices. They say gold – five hundred pounds. Take it. Kill, Kill all.
Paul: Your hear –
Andrew: Sarah is there but she sleeps – yet she scarce tasted the drugged drink, but the boy sleeps soundly and the girl above, no noise. The gold is under the bed.
John: Oh, Heaven...
Paul: Hush, or your life.

Page 90

Andrew: I have the box here, now to open it with a false key. Ah, here's the gold, it is heavy. Ah, the child wakes. The brat, it is old enough to talk. Your father's money, is it? Die, that shuts your mouth, my little critter. The others are awakened. What say my voices, 'kill all, kill all'. It's done, two thrusts, it is done. Ah, Sarah, you know all. Will you fly with me? No, then die. Mercy? I have none. I love you but you do not love me. No, it is he whose picture you wear on your bosom you love. To your heart. So now for the gold. I have blood on my hands, they are red. Who said 'murderer'? At that face at the window, it is the old gypsy. Die you. So I'll shift the blame on him...Now to hide the gold, ha! It is better than flight! I will remove it again tomorrow. Tomorrow.

Andrew goes to trap in door, and lifts up bag.

Paul: With his own mouth he has condemned himself. Now I will remove the spell that enchants him. Murderer, awake!
Andrew: Where am I here? This gold...
John: You monster. The gold for which you sold your miserable soul for, which you murdered that poor girl and my murdered innocents.
Andrew: *You have* discovered all.

Margaret enters.

Margaret: What means this?
John: It means that justice has secured her prey. Away with the murderer, to prison.
Paul: I said this old gypsy would fool you yet.

Andrew exits with the Officer. Picture, close in by the quick.

IV. Prison

Bell without tolls. **Andrew** is seen sitting on the floor, the **Governor** speaks near him.

Governor: You unhappy man. Is this your full confession?
Andrew: It is.
Governor: Have you anything more to reveal. Quick your time is short.
Andrew: No, I was tempted. Voices urged me on.
Governor: Fatal delusion.
Andrew: Oh, sir, I see it now. Say, can there be hope for such as I am?
Governor: Heaven's mercy is found beyond the grave.
Andrew: The grave, that even is denied me. My body is to be hung in chains for crows and birds of prey to devour. Oh, my poor old father. What shame have I brought on his grey house?
Governor: Your vain regrets are too late to indulge in now. Make peace with Heaven, your time is short.

The Governor exits.

Andrew: But eternity is long. 'Oh Heaven...' yet I cannot pray. Heaven's ears are closed against me. (*Bell.*) Ah, that bell again. It tolled so for her funeral now it rings my knell. The scaffold, oh, horror – and see, she is there and those innocents I slew. They bar my way to Heaven's mercy and with loud voices proclaim my eternal condemnation. Oh, those voices that urged me on to murder, to thieve...What have you led me to? See, she is there but this time alone. I do not fear your girl, I will struggle with you – hence away! I feel her bony hand clinch me, she drags me down to torturers. Oh, mercy! Mercy!

The **Governor** and **Wardens** enter. They raise **Andrew** up; he looks wildly around, as processions are forced to close in scene.

V: The Churchyard.

John and **Margaret** stand near tombstone. The inscription can be seen behind them.

John: (Alas, her reasons fled.) Think not of your sorrow or you will break your heart.
Margaret: Shush, you will wake my little ones. They sleep soundly and I soon shall see my fair haired boy and his little sisters. I have woven a garland for them - lilies, pure and fresh just like themselves. See, dear John, they call to me. Do you hear them? I do and she is with them, that faithful girl who would have died to save them. Ah, what pain is this? Is it death? No, it is release from care. Your mother has here, and has her children in her arms. I hear you that heavenly strain, it says 'forgive as we hope to be forgiven'.

Margaret falls, and dies. Scene opens tableau.
Curtain closes. The end.

Chapter 15

Theatrical Acclaim

Newspaper Cuttings

The first four newspaper snippets (1878 to 1891) are reproduced with permission of The British Newspaper Archive (www.britishnewspaperarchive.co.uk) © The British Library Board.

The Era, 17 February 1878

SEAHAM HARBOUR.
THEATRE ROYAL.—During this week we have had Mr W. Stevens in his original drama entitled *The Softy of Merrington*, in which he plays the hero, Andrew Mills. Business bad.

'Seaham Harbour. Theatre Royal – During this week we have had Mr W. Stevens in his original drama entitled 'The Softy of Merrington', in which he plays the hero, Andrew Mills. Business bad.'

Sunderland Daily Echo, 16 March 1878

LYCEUM THEATRE.
At the Lyceum Theatre last night, the romantic fairy drama "Walter the Woodcutter" was produced, followed by the "Safety of Marrington, Andrew Mills, the Homicide." The performance was well patronised by the public. To-night three grand spectacular dramas will be produced, and on Monday Mr. Fawcett Lomax will appear in the new Irish drama, "Shamus, or Speidhor-na-Glanna."

'At the Lyceum Theatre last night, the romantic fairy drama "Walter the Woodcutter" was produced, followed by the "Safety of Merrington, Andrew Mills, the Homicide." The performances were well patronised by the public...'

North and South Shields Daily Gazette, 29 March 1878

SIDDALL'S
ALHAMBRA AND AMPHITHEATRE,
Coronation Street, Mill Dam, South Shields.
Proprietor...S. B. SIDDALL.
Immense reception. Every Evening.
Mr STEPHENS, with his powerful Dramatic Company.
Grand new local Drama—Mechanical Boats—entitled
LIFE AND DEATH OF RENFORTH.
Concluding with the local Drama ANDREW MILLS,
as performed at Lyceum Theatre, Sunderland, with
great success. No advance in the prices.

'Siddall's Almabra and Amphitheatre, South Shields... Concluding with the local drama ANDREW MILLS as performed at Lyceum Theatre, Sunderland, with great success. No advance on the prices.'

Morpeth Herald, 31 October 1891

BEDLINGTON THEATRE. — This theatre was opened for the season on Friday last by a company under Mr. Wilford Stephens. The company is a powerful array of dramatic and musical talent, and well worth hearing. A start was made on Friday in the " Frozen Tarn," a tale of three lives, in which Mr. Chas. Cameron, Mr. Percy Shelley, Mr. Vernon Smithers, Mr. Fred. Hart, Mr. Wilfred Chrichton. Mr. Leeson, and Mr. Wilford Stephens took part, and Miss Carrie Henderson, Miss Summers, also played their parts well. On Monday " Help across the sea," and on Tuesday " East Lynne," was played. On Wednesday night Mr. Wilford produced one of his own dramas, entitled, " Andrew Mills or a softy of Merrington." Mr. Wilford Stephens took Andrew Mills and went through the part in a most creditable manner, being ably assisted by the whole of the company. At the conclusion of the piece, Mr. Wilford Stephens sang two comic songs which were well taken with. Mrs. Fred Hart was pianist, and no doubt during the next two months Mr. Foreman will bring good talent, and it is to be hoped he will receive good patronage.

'Bedlington Theatre. – This theatre was opened for the season on Friday last by a company under Mr Wilford Stephens. The company is a powerful array of dramatic and musical talent, and well worth hearing...On Wednesday night Mr. Wilford produced one of his own dramas, "Andrew Mills or a softy of Merrington." Mr. Wilford Stephens took Andrew Mills and went through the part in a most creditable manner, being able assisted by the whole of the company. At the conclusion of the piece, Mr. Wilford Stephens sang two comic songs which were well taken with. Mrs. Fred Hart was pianist....'

The following newspaper snippet is reproduced with permission of *Johnston Press North East.*

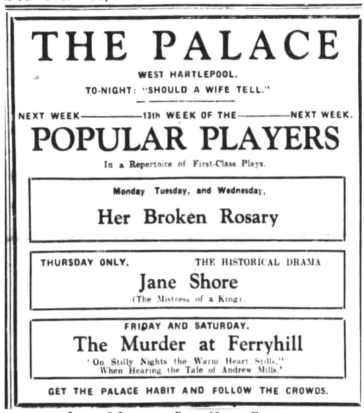

IMAGE © JOHNSTON PRESS NORTH EAST.

'The Palace. West Hartlepool. Friday and Saturday. The Murder at Ferryhill. "On Stilly Nights the Warm Heart Stills, When Hearing the Tale of Andrew Mills.'

A 140 year old review

When I discovered the location of the theatre play, I could not believe it. Here am I, an independent historian who has managed to track down one of the county's long 'lost' plays. When I purchased a photocopy of it, and it came through the post, and opened it, I was, and admit, a bit worried that I would not be able to read the original handwritten scenes. I need not have worried, although I had to modernise some of the wording, and there are tad words that I simply could not make out regardless.

The next thing was writing to the British Library and requesting if I could transcribe the play for this book, without using the actual images – that is, reproducing the actual image of the handwritten notes. They allowed it, and all fees were waived. I could not thank them enough.

The next job, and this was big, was finding the time to transcribing it from the beginning. This I managed, and it is well worth it. It is a wonderful play. The scenes are well scripted, and there are some scenes, which are particularly funny, and some scenes that were quite creepy, particularly the ending, which brings all of the scenes together. It would be interesting if, in the future, it could be performed again in public theatres, as it would be well worth the money to watch it being performed again.

The only issues that I have personally with the play are the historical accuracy. Whilst the parents' names are correct and well played, the children themselves do not actually have a part in the play (you hear of them but do not see them) and appear quite younger than what they were in real life. I suppose this was to bring in a more dramatic atmosphere, and to face it, all children of parents, regardless of their age in life, are just that, children. They are little lambs, and they never in parent's eyes get any older, when they actually do. Furthermore, there is no record of additional maids or servants belonging to John and Margaret Brass, and there has never been any historical mention of a gypsy friend to John Brass.

All this been said, and what must be understood, and I understand this now, is that in the 19th Century, all dramas had to be approved by the Lord Chamberlain office. They in turn would approve the licence for the play, suggest alterations, or decline the play entirely based on its content. They had to be suitable for families. Any theatres performing unauthorised plays would have been heavily fined.

Finally, I am extremely proud to bring this play, in its entirety, to the modern audience. The play has not been in seen in the public hands for 140 years, and has not been performed in public for well over 80 years. This would not be possible, without The British Library. Many, many, thanks.

The Stage Scenes

Having the pleasure of reading and copying the play from the original handwritten notes, this is how I imagine how the stage scenes would be set.

Act One.

Scene I. A road, stage is empty of props, except for a background canvas painting in foreground, blue and orange colours denoting twilight.

Scene II and III. Interior of farmhouse (picture below). Darker twilight colours in background canvas. Blues turning darker, and oranges turning red (through light on stage).

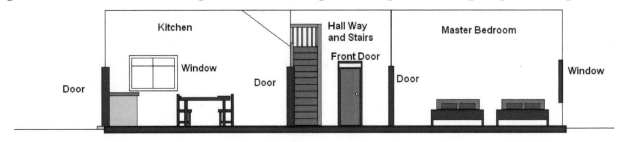

Act Two.

Scene I to III: Interior of farmhouse. Night colours. Little lights on stage except small light in kitchen to hall way, red and white light for master bedroom. Small light outside window of master bedroom.

Act Three.

Scene I. Dawn. Exterior of Kitchen. Background canvas, light turning brighter into day.

Scene II. A road, no props on stage except for a background canvas painting in foreground, blue and orange colours denoting twilight.

Scene III. Interior of farmhouse. Night colours. Little lights on stage except small light in kitchen to hall way, no lights for master bedroom. Small light outside window of kitchen window.

Scene IV. Prison, stage is empty except for grey background canvas. Small lights to promote darkness.

Scene V: Churchyard, tomb in foreground, surround by twilight colours. Canvas on background denotes inscription of tombstone.

Chapter 16
The 21st Century

The Old Mill

The Myth and the Truth

THE OLD MILL
(COURTESY OF MAUREEN ANDERSON)

There are some aspects of the murder folklore that persists to this day that the 'old mill', which stands adjacent to High Hill House, was the place where the horrible event occurred. This could be cause of its namesake – Andrew Mills and the mill. This is the final myth to dispel.

The truth is that the murders took place inside the farmhouse – High Hill House farm, and this event has nothing to do with the mill itself. Through historical research, there is no mention of a mill close to High Hill House farm prior to the 19th Century. According to the 1841 *Ordnance Survey map* of Ferryhill, the windmill was marked as 'Ferryhill Windmill (Corn)', and had about two mill cottages close by, and the user can clearly see only one road linking the mill to Merrington Road, and there is no road linking the mill to the farm. In fact, the original road to High Hill House came in from the left of what is now Ferryhill Business and Enterprise College.

On an 1861 *Ordnance Survey map* of Ferryhill, a road from the mill to the farm is shown, therefore in the 20-year period between 1841 and 1861, there was an official link made between the two buildings.

In 1921, *an Ordnance Survey map* of Ferryhill show the mill to be disused, after it was struck by lightning and crippled its foundations. No official date has yet been found when this occurred. For safety reasons, the sails were removed, as well as the rotating cap inside. The mill cottages were demolished. For years since, the mill stood alone in a field, but fenced off to prevent anyone attempting to come near it. Its derelict shape, and the fact that the walls were crippled at both sides, suggests that at some point there was an attempt to knock it down, but the process was stopped.

There was even a local horror story associated with the mill, in that if you were to run around it anticlockwise thirteen times, and call out 'Andrew Mills', the spectre of the murderer is supposed to appear, and chase the wrongdoer with his axe, and vanish when reaching the end of the dirt path, upon Merrington Road.

In 2008, the old mill was beautifully restored with an adjoining house and was sold by Dowen Housing for just over £350,000. 'The Windmill' property is now a spacious family home with 4 bedrooms, an ensuite toilet and shower, a family bathroom, a lounge and a joint kitchen and dining, and is currently in residence, with no ghosts.

The Devil Within Film

IMAGE © CAPTURE FILMS, NEWTON AYCLIFFE

In 2007, Sedgefield Borough Council (now Durham County Council) commissioned the 30-minute film at the cost of £20,000. Six young actors from Endeavour Training, a charity that supports young people who are not in full time education, training or employment, teamed up with professional actors, and brought in Capture Films in Newton Aycliffe to help film it.

The film was premiered at Bishop Auckland Town Hall on 23rd April 2007, and shown across parts of the south of Durham afterwards. I was fortunate enough to watch it during its tour, and to obtain a copy of it on DVD.

The film surrounds the same myth that the murders took place in the old mill, and the Devil instructed Andrew Mills to undertake the task. Whist the murder took place outside of the farmhouse and therefore not historically accurate, the film is incredible, and is available on Youtube by exclusive permission of Capture Films.

High Hill House Farm

Kill All, Kill All, a book by Craig McNish

The murders of 1683 still hold fascination to anyone who enjoys a murder mystery. This fascination is well represented in an Amazon Kindle novel written by Mr. Craig McNish, called *'Kill All, Kill All'*. It is based on the idea that Andrew Mills is brought back to life in the 21st Century, but still has the devil torturing his soul and telling him what to do. I shall not spoil the rest.

Broom Mill Day Spar Ltd

This book would not be complete without mentioning Broom Mill Day Spar Ltd (*www.broommilldayspar.co.uk*), a family company of the farm, set up near to High Hill House, which provides luxury, beauty and personal care at friendly and good prices.

It is interesting that how a place of murder can also be a place for relaxation and good heath, but it works really well. It is also fascinating that such areas can pursue good health. Remember the tale of Andrew Mills' Stob and how its wood was good for curing toothache, and other minor ailments? It is the same principle. Perhaps there is some hard truth in maiden's tales.

Finally, the legend of the ghostly tale of *'his wild cries can still be heard in the area near the farmhouse at new year'*, is simply a legend, and is not true at all. The farmhouse is resident to a private family, who are well aware of the house's misfortunate and do not like to speak of it to most people. Luckily, I had the good fortune of speaking to one of the farm's residents, and she informs me that she has never come across any sort of spectral apparition or heard any sort of ghostly moans or cries in or around the farmhouse. If it were, it would probably be some local teenagers, trying to bring back the ghost of Andrew Mills to chase them, and after waiting, realising that after 300 years, the ghosts of the past are long since dead...

Chapter 17
'...There are more things in heaven and earth...'

If you still think that the murderous event of 1683 was only due to human drama and mental instability instead of diabolical influence, think again. This chapter examines the most superstitious aspects of the story.

N.B. I would like to express that this information does not represent all living persons or organisation today, but only how all of this information combined may have had some diabolical influence in the original event.

Numbers

The number three

The number 3 is very significant in religion. It is the first perfect number and is a number of perfect trinity, unity and power. God, Son, and the Holy Ghost. Mother, Father, and Child. Prophet, priest, and King. However, demonologists believe that forces of evil twist sacred numbers to their own devices, such as the Devil, the Anti-Christ and the False Prophet.

- The year was 1683 (n.s.) when the murder happened.
- There were three children murdered. There shared birthdays on the same day when they were murdered. This is linked to when King Herod ordered all the first sons to be murdered, after the birth of Christ.
- They were murdered on the 25th (the number between 2 and 5 equals 3)
- Andrew Mills denied three times that he murdered them (like Saint Peter denied Jesus Christ when He was arrested and brought before the Roman court.)

The number thirteen

The number 13 is important in Christianity. 13 usually represents The Last Supper in which Christ and his twelve apostles shared in the Lord's last words of wisdom, the wine representing Christ's blood, and the bread, representing Christ's body. However, Judas Iscariot did not partake and instead betrayed Jesus to the Chief Priests for thirty silver coins. Most people consider 13 to be very unlucky, particularly on a Friday, although some people can be born on Friday 13th, and are considered very lucky.

- The children were buried on the 26th (13 x 2). It was also a Friday.
- The number 13 appears right next to their burial record.
- High Hill House stands 184 meters above sea level. (1+8+4 = 13)

The number six, nine, and eighteen.

The number six in Christianity represents imperfection, and the creation of man in the universe. It is also a twisted number as it can easily become the number 9. Three sixes or eighteen is believed to represent the Devil or the Anti-Christ upon the earth.

- If Andrew Mills were 17 years old when he murdered the Brass children in 1683, then his year of birth would be approximately 1666.
- Andrew Mills is believed to have committed the murders in the evening between 6pm and 9 pm.
- High Hill House Farm, the land surrounding the farmhouse, is 180 meters above sea level (18 can be seen quite clearly).

Days

Sunday, the day of the Sabbath

Sunday, or the Sabbath Day, is referred to in the Bible as the Lord's Day of rest, following His creation of the World and Man. Traditionally, people born on a Sunday are considered to be beautiful (both within the mind and without in features), energetic, law-abiding, and happy.

- The Birth of Jane Brass, who is considered a hero of the original story, was calculated to be on a Sunday (through calculations via www.timeanddate.com and Calculator.net). She was also baptised on a Sunday.

'Sad' Wednesday

Wednesday is considered the day that Jesus Christ and his disciplines sat down for the Last Supper. It is also the day that Jesus was betrayed. People born of this day are considered full of woe, because of the actions of Judas' betrayal.

- The Birth of John Brass, the brother to Jane Brass, is calculated to be on a Wednesday (again via the above websites). He is believed to be part of the antagonist towards Andrew Mills, which led to his sisters and his own demise.
- Andrew Mills was 'hung in chains' on Wednesday 15th August 1683.

'Bloody' Thursday

Thursday is mostly considered the day when Jesus Christ stood trial at the Roman Court, before his crucifixion on a Friday – 'Good Friday'. It is considered the day that he was whipped by the Roman soldiers and a crown of thorns was placed on his head. Some people now theorise that Christ's trial and crucifixion took place on a Thursday, which then allowed three nights before His resurrection – 'Easter Sunday'.

- The birth of Elizabeth Brass, the youngest child, is calculated to be on a Thursday. (Again as above). Apart from her own sister, Elizabeth would also be considered holy, as her powerful intervention on the day of the murder nearly saved her life.
- The children were murdered on a Thursday.

'Unlucky' Friday

Friday, according to tradition is the day of Christ's crucifixion, although there is some debate about this. Superstition prevails that Friday is considered the worst days of the week, as evil is at its most strongest, particularly the day happens to fall on the 13th.

- The children were buried on a Friday, 26th January 1683 (n.s).

Astrology

First Quarter Moon

The First Quarter Moon is often called 'crisis moon' or 'crisis in action'. It is the time when there is dramatic crisis within the world, untold actions, and unready preparations for a new beginning.

- According to the website www.timeanddate.com, on the 25th of January 1683 (n.s.), the date of the murder, the moon was in its first quarter.

Animals

Although animals do not show themselves prominently within this story, there are animal elements within the myths that are quite important to Christian symbols.

The Devil in the Hallway

According to a persistent legend, when Andrew Mills left Elizabeth, the youngest child, alive for a moment, and entered the hallway leading to the bedrooms, he met a creature, *like a fierce wolf with red fiery eyes, its two legs were like those of a stag, and its body resembled an eagle, and was supplied with two enormous wings'*. In order to look at this closely, we need to break it down.

- The wolf is considered the most evil symbol in Christianity. The Devil in mythology is often portrayed as animal and wolf like.
- Any spirit that has 'red fiery eyes' would be considered demonic in nature.

- The eagle and the stag are powerful good Christian symbols. The eagle represents hope and strength, and salvation, and the stag represents authority and resurrection (the antlers above the head – the cap of God, linking earth and heaven; and how the antlers die, fall off, and grow back). The Devil and demons tend to mock Christian symbols and flip the images over.

Dogs howling

Within superstition, any dog that is seen or heard howling without provocation is an ill omen, and often denotes death, either upcoming or recently past.

- One popular legend has the Brass parents returning home, and their horse stop suddenly after it hears the unhealthy howls of a nearby dog.

A Poem

I devised the following poem some years ago, and I think is still relevant to the story.

1.
Sixteen Hundred and Eighty Three,
January the Twenty-fifth, that day –
On Thursday night when parents were out,
Their Children did pass away.

2.
At Brasse Farm, near Ferry Hill,
Were Elizabeth, John and Jane,
With their father's servant Andrew Mills
In the house was left those in.

3.
Murther was done, Andrew Mills
To Ferry Hill slowly speed,
Near Nine o' the Clock, he met some troops
And told of the horrid deed.

4.
The troops seized Mills and took him hence
where Master and Dame were at.
John and Margaret Brasse were with friends
When Andrew stated that:

5.
"Our Johnny and Jany are both Kill'd,
And young Elizabeth too."
Though upon seeing blood on his clothes,
Said the Mother, "Villain, it was thou."

6.
Straight to the house, people in plenty ran,
And Andrew being seized came,
But oh, when to the house, the sight they saw –
They knew who was to blame.

7.

In a room, the Children were found
All mangled, cold, and dead.
Their skulls were cleft, their throats were cut,
And were lying in their bed.

8.

They searched Mills' pocket, they found his knife,
which was smothered all with blood,
And the two axe which were laid on the floor
Was covered from steel to wood.

9.

"I deny the Fact that I did this",
Andrew Mills did explain.
"It was not me, but two men that came,
Who did this barbarous thing."

10.

A Coroner was called, and a Jury was formed
And examined the servant Andrew:
"Was it thee who kill'd these children three,
And claims it was not thou."

11.

" I deny the Fact that I did this",
Again said the felon.
So the Jury withdrew, and the Coroner desired
To speak to Andrew alone:

12.

"I will befriend thee, and save your life,
If thou confess your sin."
So Andrew thought and did refrain,
"I did the Children in."

13.

Now, Some folks believe this was not the case
That Andrew engaged that act
For he stated that two men to the house did come,
And committed this horrid act.

14.

Howsoever, there is little source
To give Andrew Mills appraise.
For the past did state he'd confessed this crime,
From voices which made him craze.

15.

So to Durham Gaol Andrew went,
And there he had remained,
'Til day of trial, when Judge announced
For Andrew to be Hung and Chained.

16.

I believe at Durham it was the place
For Andrew to be hang'd.
With binded rope, his breath did cease;
His body swung in the wind.

17.

Few days past, troops took him down
From the rope he was there still.
His body was tarred and iron chained
And brought back to Ferry Hill.

18.

August the Fifteenth of that year –
His stob and cage erect,
And none dared travel on Durham Road
Especially in the night.

19.

Now, some folks say, this was not the case
That in Durham he did cease,
But at Ferry Hill, after several days,
Our God did give him peace.

20.

His stob remained on Durham Road –
A sight for all around,
Until Eighteen Hundred and four times ten,
When it was taken down.

21.

In Merrington churchyard, the Children lay
Still resting in their sleep.
For those who visit to this site, will have
A weathered tomb to meet.

22.

Now, none can say why he kill'd the bairns,
But some folks today have saith,
"That the Devil came to Andrew Mills,
And he axed the Children to death."

23.

I pity thee, Andrew Mills,
For thou own devil'd state.
If voices heard and visions saw,
No comfort did thou seek.

24.

And Woe to thee Little Ones,
Elizabeth, John, and Jane.
In Devil hands that caused thou death,
And In God Hands thou art in.

25.

And note to those who doth read this,
A fair warning I wish to say –
"If thou commit a blackest deed
The Devil will take thee away."

Epilogue

Remember...

Respect, Forgive,
Love and Live

Whether you believe that the murders were committed out of some insane impulse, or whether you believe that the devil really told Andrew Mills to kill, the end result was inevitable. The children were murdered, and Andrew was hung for it.

For over 300 years, Andrew Mills has been recorded as a malicious, intent, and careless monster. Perhaps he was, or perhaps he was innocent all along and simply blamed, tried and executed for the murder, as there was not the modern evidence that could support his case otherwise. He paid the price for it.

Now surely, in the 21st Century, we must understand that Andrew was a human being, a person of flesh and blood, who had feelings like the rest of us, who loved, and wanted love, and may have been bullied because of his mentality or his status. Such neglect of his character could have led to his feelings of mistrust and anger to a family who he had to serve several years as an apprentice. Should we continuously blame him for his actions? Were those actions his alone? We will never know the real truth, but the morals of this story are simple.

- Treat everyone with humility and respect.
- Always forgive others, as you would expect others to forgive you.
- Allow people to love and live, regardless of how long you love and live.
- As Jesus was nailed to His Cross, he pleaded with Heaven, *'Forgive them Father, they do not know what they do.'*

To put our love in God, we must know the Devil is real.

The Devil's greatest trick on mankind is to believe that he does not exist...

The world is a paradox of good and evil, right and wrong. As human beings, it is considerably hard for us to not break some of the Ten Commandments in our everyday lives. Even in this modern world, there are those who break these acts of God without any love, care or humanity in their hearts. Should we treat those badly who wrong us? In small ways, yes, but we should not kill each other mercilessly. *'To gain peace, one must prepare for war'.* The war with the devil is an ongoing batter that will continue to threaten mankind until eternity, as long as man shall live. But we must live, and live better. We must become better people than we already are. We must stop prejudice and hate, for these will doom us all.

Was Andrew Mills a form of the devil, whose sole mission was become employed and carry out a heinous act, or was it the Devil whose evil influence brought about the unfortunate environment and mental ability, that the young servant could not abstain from. Did the Devil come to Ferryhill? He did, one way or the other...

...Lest we forget.

If you ever find yourself in the Churchyard of Kirk Merrington, take a few moments and stand near the tombstone of the fallen children. Pray for them. Let them find happiness in the knowledge that in their deaths, mankind can still be reprieved from evil. Remember these words.

'Here lies the Bodies

Of JOHN, JANE and ELIZABETH

Children of

JOHN and MARGARET BRASS

Who were murdered, the 25th of January 1683,

By Andrew Mills, their father's servant,

For which he was   hung in chains

Reader, remember, sleeping

We were slain;

& Here we sleep till we must

Rise again

Whose sheddeth man's blood by

Man shall his blood be shed

Thou shall do no murther.'

The End.

Bibliography

Used as Reference Only

- Allardryce, Nicole A History of English Drama, 1660 to 1990, Volume Five, 19th Century Drama, 1959;
- Ashleigh, Leonard R.N. The Complete Book of Devils and Demons, 1996
- British Library A most Horrid and Barbarous Murder Committed in the County of Palatine in Durham, near Ferry-Hill, (Neg; PB.Mic.44943);
- Burn, Richard, The Justice of the Peace, and Parish Officer, 1758;
- Capture Films *'The Devil Within'* film;
- Durham Cathedral Library Petition regarding quarrying in or around Ferryhill, DCD/K/LP7/9 – 15
- Durham University, Archives and Special Collections The Diary of Jacob Bee, XE 942.06 BEE; In the County of Palatine in Durham near Ferry-Hill, SB+0454;
- Fraser, Antonia *King Charles II*, 1992;
- Guiley, Rosemary Ellen The Encyclopaedia of Vampires, Werewolves, and Other Monsters, 2005;
- Ledger, Edward The Era Almanac, Dramatic and Musical, no date;
- McNish, Craig *Kill All, Kill All*, 2013;
- Meiklejohn, Prof. A New History of England and Great Britain, no date;
- Milton, John *Paradise Lost*, 1667;
- Nixon, Philip Exploring Durham History, 1998;
- Roud, Steve The Penguin Guide to the Superstitions of Britain and Ireland, 2003;
- Spencer, Charles *Killers of the King*, 2014.

Images / Text Used by Permission

- Anderson, Maureen *Foul Deeds and Suspicious Deaths in and around Durham*, 2003. Picture of the old mill, page 19. Colour photo sent by exclusive permission;
- DeviantArt.com: Maz Fentiman (*Blackstar2302*), Nathan Cox and Josh Fritz (*The-Screaming-Cat*), Graeme Pattison (*Newcastlemale*);
- Durham County Council, Clayport Library The County of Palatine in Durham near Ferry-Hill, 1682;
- Durham County Record Office, D/XP 77; EP/MER 1; EP/MER 2, EP/MER 34;
- Malkin, John *Ferryhill Facts*, community newspaper. April / May 1989;
- The British Library Board, British Newspaper Archive Website, *snippets of various newspapers dated 1878 and 1891;*
- Johnston Press North East, snippet of newspaper dated 1930;
- The British Library Board, Lord Chamberlain Play Collection, *Andrew Mills, Legend of Spennymoor,* (*Add MS 53169 L*), Licensed August 1876.

Snippet Information

- Author Unknown. The Monthly Chronicle of North Country Lore and Legends: Volume One, article on 'Andrew Mills', 1887;

- Author Unknown. The Monthly Chronicle of North Country Lore and Legends: Volume Two, article on 'Waterton at Tudhoe', 1888;

- Billings, Robert Architectural Antiquities of Durham, 1846;

- Chamberlain, Edward Angliae Notitia: or, The Present State of England: the First Part, 1676 (Google Books);

- Clevell, R; Mortlock, H; Robinson, J The New State of England Under their Majesties K. William and Q. Mary, 1693 (Google Books);

- Dodds, James The History of the Urban District of Spennymoor, 1897;

- Durham Cathedral Library, Allan, George *Collectanea Dunelmensla*,

- Hartshorne, Albert *Hanging in Chains*, 1891;

- Hodgson, John Crawford Six North Country Diaries, the Diary of Jacob Bee, no date;

- James VI and I, *Demonologie*, 1599;

- James VI and I, *King James Bible*, 1611;

- Longstaff, William The History and Antiquities of the Parish of Darlington, 1909

- Scobell, Henry An Ordnance for enabling the Judge, or Judges, of the Northern Circuit, to hold Assizes and Gaol Deliveries at Durham, 1654, Durham County Council Library Collection;

- Shakespeare, William The Tragedy of Hamlet, Prince of Denmark, 1603;

- Stubbes, Phillip *The Anatomie of Abuses*, 1580 (Google Books);

- Surtees, Robert The History and Antiquities of the County Palatine of Durham, Volume 3, 1823;

- Sykes, John Local Records; or Historical Register of Remarkable Events which have occurred in Northumberland and Durham...Volume One, 1866;

- Weever, John Antient Funeral Monuments, of Great-Britain, Ireland, and the islands adjacent, 1631 (Google Books);

- Wells, George Certain Sermons or Homilies Appointed to be Read in Churches In the Time of Queen Elizabeth of Famous Memory: and now Reprinted for the use of Private Families, 1687 (Google Books).

Websites (as reference)

- Broom Mill Day Spar Ltd (*www.broommilldayspar.co.uk*);

- Calculator.net;

- Durham University, Pictures in Print website;

- Durham University Probate Records - DPR/I/1/1722/B12/1-2, DPR/I/1/1839/L14/1-2;

- Findmypast.com, *Census Records*;

- FreeREG.org.uk; *Parish Records*;

- Google Books;
- The National Archives online catalogue - *DURH* 17/1/16; *DURH* 17/1/17; *ASSI* 44/3;
- Schizophrenia.com;
- Timeanddate.com;
- Wilkipedia: Statute of Artificers 1563, Poor Law Acts 1601.

About the Author
Darrell S. Nixon

I am an independent historian and researcher into mysterious and murderous events in County Durham, and other supernatural events.

This is my first publication into the dark and rather diabolical history into County Durham, and I thought of no better way into introduce my work than the oldest crime in Ferryhill.

Did the Devil really come to Ferryhill, or was it a crime of passion or despair, or was it simply an insane impulse, maybe brought on schizophrenia? It would probably been the latter, however it is interesting to find unusual characteristics which may link the murders to the doings of the Devil and demonology, and to the times which the event took place. This is why my book heading is entitled *"Demonic County Durham."*

I hope in the end of 2016 to bring about a new book called *"Demonic County Durham: The Vengeful Spirit of Lumley near Durham, 1630"*, and in 2017, *"Demonic County Durham: A Diabolical Possession at Edmundbyers near Durham, 1641."*

I sincerely hope that you enjoyed this book, and I will endeavour to keep you interested in further strange and sinister aspects of County Durham's history

Again, thank you very much for your support.

Most Kindest Regards,

Darrell S. Nixon
www.DarrellSNixon.com

Printed in the USA
CPSIA information can be obtained
at www.ICGtesting.com
LVHW060417060224
771000LV00002B/26